Time Jockey Chronicles

Volume I: 2007-2008

Written by Joe Castillo

Edited by Ms. Silvia Alvarado

A collection of articles written by the author, Joe Castillo, under the pen name '*Time Jockey*' and published in 2007 -2008

Net sales of this book will be distributed to the Native Sons of the Golden West Historical Preservation Foundation and the Matt Castillo Memorial Scholarship Fund

0

In Dedication

This book is dedicated to my family and friends who were there when I needed them most and continue to be there for me as I reflect on my own history. It is especially dedicated to the following special people in my life:

- *My mom, Victoria, my inspiration in life who taught me to respect and appreciate our history while sharing her memories of her 94 years;*

- *My son, Joey, who took me on a number of adventures which I would have never gone on without his persuasion, and for which I am forever grateful;*

- *My late son, Matt, whose laugh and humor brought me boundless joy and happiness, and who will forever remain in a very special and cherished place in my life and my heart;*

- *My special lady, Silvia, who has been there for me during the best and worst of times and is my perfect soulmate and even better friend.*

Disclaimer

The information presented in this book is based on historical facts and is the author's own interpretation of the facts. It is the author's intent to provide the reader with an insightful look at history, through historical facts, focused research, individual accounts and legendary tales. His source of information includes published books, newspaper articles, personal interviews, multimedia presentations, individual experiences and other miscellaneous resources. Any misrepresentations of presented facts and statements are strictly and purely unintentional.

First printing 2015, California, USA

ISBN: 978-0-996-3424-0-7

TABLE OF CONTENTS

Chapter 1: 'Time Jockey' – *Riding Through History* – By Joe Castillo (10-07-07)

Let Me Introduce Myself ...... Well, hello and welcome to 'Time Jockey', a column focused on the history of the San Gabriel Valley. The valley is filled with a wealth of historical information, some of which you may be aware of and some of which you may not. But if you take a little time, you'll notice it's all around us, from the cities we live in, to the street we live on and the places which surround us. This column will look at the multitude of historical places, persons, organizations and events which helped to shape this area and our communities..... You may be wondering why this column is called 'Time Jockey'. Well, it's because, I'll be taking you through different time frames, moving from one event, location and area to another. I won't be writing long articles which consist of multiple parts or chapters on a historical event or person but I will be writing short articles on interesting historical facts, persons, statements, resources, events and dates. In addition, I'll also be including stories, legends and tales, which add more color to our history. ..... Many of the sources used in this column will be from books, publications, records and documents written in the 1900's, as well as more recently written works. And of course, as with all historical research, there may be a difference of facts and opinions, so we will try and present a fair interpretation of all past historical occurrences.... So come along and enjoy the ride and like a good jockey who guides his horse through the race and drives him to the finish line, I'll try and guide you through the past by making this column as interesting, informational and humorous as I can so that you might be able to better appreciate and learn more about our local history. Hope you enjoy the column! ... ***Town for Sale*** ... Temple City was originally named Town of Temple in 1923, and then shortened to Temple before the name of Temple City was adopted in 1928..... Walter P. Temple, the founder of the Town of Temple, along with a group of investors purchased the 285-acre parcel to build and design a community to house 5,000 people... According to the realty brochure trying to draw potential buyers, lots on Las Tunas were on sale for $200 each, home sites for $1,200

5

and half-acre lots cost $1,950. ..... **_A Mission is Founded!_** ....Mission San Gabriel was founded on September 4th, 1771 and recently celebrated its 236th anniversary. ... The location of the original site is in present day Montebello, at the corner of San Gabriel Blvd. and Lincoln Ave.... In 1775, due to the unpredictable river flow in that area, the site was moved to a more stable location, approximately 5 miles north to its present site in San Gabriel.... However, it wasn't until 1791 that construction began on the present day mission structure.... Fourteen years later in 1805, construction of the Mission San Gabriel was finally complete!.... **_Let The Lions Roar!_**..... In 1923, Charles Gay, opened Gay's Lion Farm in El Monte.... The farm was home to approximately 200 African Lions, who were used in Hollywood movies as well as a tourist attraction.... The farm was open from 1925 until 1942, and during that time students from El Monte High School became so attached to the lions that the school adopted the lion as their mascot.... From time to time, Charles Gay would lend one of his small baby lions to the school as a 'live' mascot to be used for school events.... If you go by El Monte High School today, you'll see a statue of a golden lion sitting at the front entrance of the school.... Coincidentally, this is the same statue which was located in front of Gay's Lion Farm until 1942.... **_Watch Out For The Needles!_** .... Las Tunas Blvd. was named by Walter P. Temple, during the development of the Town of Temple (Temple City)..... The Temple Family were parishioners at the Mission San Gabriel, which at that time was encircled with a cactus path or barrier that extended from the Mission, north to the dirt road where present day Las Tunas is and south back to the mission..... The barrier kept out wild animals, unruly natives and protected the Mission from any type of attack..... The cactus plants produce a small prickly fruit pod called a '*tuna*', which is edible but must be prepared with great care....When Temple designed his town, Town of Temple, and named the streets, he used the name of Las Tunas (The Tunas) for the main east-west thoroughfare... **_Farewell To A Legend ..._** John Henry, the ultimate competitive racehorse, died at the age of 32 on Monday October 8th. The gelding thoroughbred won Horse of the Year honors in 1981 and 1984, and was the first two-time winner of the prestigious Santa Anita Handicap winning in 1981 and 1982. His racing career lasted from 1977 through 1984, and he retired as the all-time money earner with $6,591,860. He may have been the most popular horse to ever run at Santa Anita, and he never let his fans down. The roar of the fans as John Henry came thundering down the stretch in the 1981 and 1982 Santa Anita Handicap may have been loudest I have ever heard at Santa Anita…. ***Places To Visit….*** The Ramona Museum, located in the historic district of San Gabriel, offers an assortment of early California artifacts, paintings and documents. Some of the more interesting objects include the horse carriage which Capt. John Fremont rode in following the US-Mexico War, a copy of the first map of the pueblo of Los Angeles drawn by the surveyor Ord, and the collection of Los Angeles County Sheriff Eugene Biscailuz…. The museum is under the direction of Ramona Parlor #109, a member of the Native Sons of the Golden West, which was established in 1887 to preserve the history of California. It is located at 339 S. Mission Rd, San Gabriel, 91776, across the street from the Mission Playhouse and the San Gabriel Grapevine. Admission is Free and it is open to the public and especially children. The hours of the museum are Saturdays from 1-4 PM. Call 626-289-0034 for more information… ***That's All Folks!*** …. If you have an interesting story regarding our local history, please send it to me and we'll so our best to include it in future columns.

Chapter 2: 'Time Jockey' – *Historical Haunts* - By Joe Castillo (10/14/07)

Bringing Life to Savannah Cemetery …Savannah Memorial Park, located at Mission Rd. and Encinitas Ave. in Rosemead, dates back to 1850 and is the final resting place of over 3,000 persons including many of the early pioneers of El Monte and Rosemead…. In the early 1850's, El Monte was a very busy place as the terminus of the Santa Fe Trail. Settlers had reached their destination and were no longer interested in seeking gold or traveling further west for fortune and fame. They had found a place with an abundance of water, rich soil for growing crops and enough natural resources to sustain their lives and survive. Two rivers, the San Gabriel and the Rio Hondo, flowed around a grassy, treeless plain providing a higher standing area of land. Known as the *savannah,* the area was used as a cemetery as agreed to by El Monte settlers and ranch owner Henry Dalton of Rancho San Francisquito…… Early El Monte Pioneers John W. Broaded, John Guess, Asa Ellis and James D. Durfee were buried in the cemetery.   The cemetery is still active today and may be used as a final resting place for those wishing to be buried there….. Over the years it has become more and more difficult to maintain and operate the park. General funds provided through donations and community contributions have been used for the day-to-day operation of the facility but many of the grave sites are in need of extensive repair and restoration. [In addition, the previous management of the cemetery struggled with these growing issues and eventually interest in Savannah deteriorated…]But thanks to a new board of directors of the El Monte Cemetery Association, the City of Rosemead, community and business leaders and the caring and generous people of the Rosemead-El Monte area, a new and exciting effort to save Savannah Memorial Park has been initiated…. Halloween Oktoberfest, a street fair with food, arts, crafts, vendors, refreshments, a raffle, carnival and haunted house, will be held on October 27th from 10AM – 9PM, at Rosemead Park, corner of Mission Rd. and Encinitas Ave. in the City of Rosemead.   Volunteers of the Savannah Memorial Park, which is located adjacent to Rosemead Park and the fair itself, will offer tours……. Proceeds received from the fair will be used to help preserve the cemetery, and just as important the community will become more aware of the historical significance of Savannah and bond together to continue efforts to save and restore one of the oldest Protestant cemeteries in Southern California. …. Everyone is welcome so come on out, have fun and help save Savannah...

Derby Chills …. I recently went to the Derby in Arcadia for dinner and was mesmerized with the abundance of horse racing artifacts on display…. The Derby was owned by Hall Of Fame jockey George Woolf, who raced at Santa Anita from 1928 until his death in 1946. In 1939, Woolf rode the great Seabiscuit to a 2-length victory over Triple Crown winner War Admiral in the 'Race of the Century', one of horse racing greatest match races….. In 1946, Woolf suffered a fatal injury when he was thrown from his mount, Pleasure Me, while riding at Santa Anita. … Following his death, his wife eventually sold the restaurant along with all of Woolfs' memorabilia, to new owners, where it is displayed for all Derby patrons and horse racing fans to view…. While riding at Santa Anita, Wolfe would stay in an upstairs room at the restaurant in order to manage his business investment while continuing to ride during the day…. There are stories that Woolfs' spirit still lives today in the Derby, at the place where he lived and close to the place where he died. While viewing the contents of the beautiful display cases at the restaurant, including the Calumet Farms racing silks that Woolf wore the day of his death, patrons have felt a 'cool breath' down their necks. Turning and seeing no one, it just may be an icy remembrance from George Woolf, who was also known as the 'Ice Man'…. It should be noted that the Prime Rib was excellent, as well as the entire dinner, service and evening, even if George was among us…. ***You'll Be Staying in Room 120*** …. The Aztec Hotel, located on historic Route 66 in Monrovia, is the home to some unexplained sightings…. Built in 1924, by architect Robert Stacy-Judd who was inspired by the Aztec and Mayan cultures, it has been a hotel, speakeasy and bordello. Starting in the 1930's, numerous Hollywood stars have stayed in the Aztec as guests, including Clark Gable, Spencer Tracy, Gene Kelly and Frank Sinatra…. According to researchers, a woman died in Room 120 after falling backwards and striking her head against a heater… Shortly thereafter, all heaters on the same floor as Room 120 no longer worked. Even after the heaters were repaired, hotel customers reported being 'chilled to the bone'…. A different story has also been told about the sightings. In 1929, Jerri Lynn, also known as 'Kitty', committed suicide in Room 120 after a romance went sour. The room was located above the basement which during the Prohibition era was used as a speakeasy. Sightings of Kitty's specter have been observed in the basement bathroom, the hall and corridor around Room 120 and the stairs leading to the haunted room …. The sightings have always described the same image, a tall, beautiful 25-year old girl, with light-colored hair wearing a wide brim hat. She is frequently seen in the corridor around Room 120 before disappearing…. The bathroom in the basement has been known to be so cold as to be freezing, even when the air conditioning in the rest of hotel was either broken or powered off and it was over a hundred degrees outside…. **_Lost in the Playhouse_** …. The San Gabriel Mission Playhouse is rumored to have some friendly spirits inside as well as within its walls…. According to former stage manager Rick Gardner, who took over the position from his father Rulon, the playhouse has been home to spirits who either helped build or maintained the facility…. In the late 1920's, construction of the playhouse began on the grand auditorium. Cement was used throughout the building and numbers of workers were needed to prepare, pour, stir and set the mixture. Skilled and non-skilled help were hired to perform the hard, labor intensive jobs…. One story states that three workers were caught in the fast-drying cement. Rescuers worked hard to free two of the three workers, but they could not extract the other worker in time. A priest was called in to perform the last rites and today he remains entombed within the stage-left walls of the playhouse, a permanent resident of the structure… Years later, a séance made contact with a spirit who had died a violent death but may have worked at the playhouse during his life. Research identified Marcus Aguilar, a former custodian, who died in an auto accident on the way to Las Vegas… Nicknamed 'Uncle John', he has been seen in later years in the rafters by people who identified him from pictures taken of Aguilar, describing even the same clothes he's wearing in the picture…. According to Gardner, the spirits are friendly and on occasion may have protected workers, performers and patrons when objects mysteriously fell or something went wrong…… Of course, these are only stories, but maybe the next time you're in the playhouse you may catch yourself looking a little longer at the Stage-left walls and the ceiling rafters…. ***Ghost Town***… In 1887, the town of Lordsburg was founded near present day Pomona by Pasadena developer Isaac W. Lord. Lord had persuaded the Santa Fe to stop there and subsequently built the 130-room Lordsburg Hotel. He also held real estate auctions to sell property in Lordsburg, but the real estate boom had already ended…. The never-used Lordsburg Hotel was sold to members of the German Baptist Brethren Church, and converted into Lordsburg College… After Lords' death, the town changed its name to La Verne in 1917, and Lordsburg College became the University of La Verne…. ***Final Resting Place….*** In the early 1850's, the pueblo of Los Angeles was a collection of buildings and adobe houses. Streets were nothing more than dirt roads used by the early settlers to travel with their horses and wagons. The names of streets were based upon their significance to city life and the people of Los Angeles…. One of the streets, *Calle de Eternidad*, started at the Old Mission Church of Los Angeles, otherwise known as '*Nuestra Senora Reina de Los Angeles*' (Our Lady Queen of Angels). Now known as North Broadway, the street means Road to Eternity and went straight up the hill to the local cemetery, close to the present day site of Cathedral High School. Incidentally, Cathedral High School's mascot is the Phantoms…. ***Upcoming Events***… Pio Pico State Historical Park will have a Living History Day October 27th from 11 AM – 3 PM. Call the park at (562) 695-1217 or go to www.piopico.org for more information…. Charles Lyons, Director of Public Relations of the San Gabriel Mission, will present a lecture on the history of the mission on October 29th at 7:30 PM, at the Southwestern Academy, 2800 Monterey Road, San Marino. Lyons will speak at the meeting of the San Marino Historical Association, admission is free. Call (626) 304-

9375 for more information.... ***Final Quotes*** ... *"The Past is not dead history, it is the living material out of which man makes himself and builds the future"*, Rene Dubos......

Chapter 3:   'Time Jockey' - *Veterans In Our History* – By Joe Castillo (11-03-07)

Saluting Our Veterans … Sunday November 11th marks the Veterans Day Holiday. Originally recognized as Armistice Day in 1938, and changed to Veterans Day in 1954, it was established to honor those who gave their time and lives serving in America's military…. America has been involved in 100 conflicts since the Revolutionary War in 1776, with men and women serving our country, either home or abroad, to protect our precious freedom ….. Throughout the nation and southland, America will honor its veterans… Ceremonies will be held, speeches will be made, flags will be saluted and our veterans will be the center of attention, the honored guests. …. This will be their special day and rightfully so, but everyday we should be thankful for the sacrifices the veterans have made to keep us at home safe and protected …. Every day we should celebrate Veterans Day! …. This issue will recognize a few of the veterans who served in conflicts from 1812 through the Iraq War and have either settled, lived or died here in the San Gabriel Valley…. *War of 1812*… Wiley R. Wilson, born in 1800 and died in 1878, served as a drummer at the age of 12 in the war against the British. He is buried in Rosemead at Savannah Cemetery …. *U.S. – Mexico War*… Thomas Alexander Mayes, born in the South, went to medical school in Philadelphia where he graduated from Thomas Jefferson Medical School…. After graduation, Mayes enlisted in the U.S. Army, where he served in the West with the U.S. Calvary as a doctor for 3 years during the War with Mexico. … After his service, Mayes settled in Santa Fe, New Mexico, where he met his future wife-to-be but he had to travel 1,000 miles to get a commitment from her…. She left Santa Fe without him and traveled west to El Monte with the second group of settlers to ever travel by wagon across the Santa Fe Trail…. Wasting no time, Mayes joined the third party and traveled to El Monte, where he proposed to his future wife… They settled in El Monte, where Mayes became one of the first doctors in the area. They built the first wooden house in El Monte on Lexington Ave…. Eventually, Dr.Mayes would go on and become the Los Angeles County Coroner …. *American Civil War:*

**Union Army** … Corporal Louis Anderson, enlisted in Company D, 16th U.S. Infantry in 1861. Anderson participated in the following battles: Shiloh, Stone River, Chickamauga, Buzzards Roost, Siege of Corinth, Hoover's Gap, Mission Ridge and was in the Georgia Campaign under Major General William Tecumseh Sherman … Anderson was discharged in August 1864, settled in Alhambra, where he died on February 28, 1906... _**Confederate Army**_ …. Colonel William Henry Stephens, 6th Tennessee Infantry Regiment of Confederate States Army, was born at Havre De Grace, Maryland on May 2, 1816 and died in San Gabriel March 3, 1887... _**World War I**_…. Sergeant Joseph L. Kauffman, Company 'C', 364th Infantry, 91st Division, A.E.F, died on September 26, 1918, at the age of 22, at the Argonne Forest, France, in defense of democracy... His good friend, Walter P. Temple, would finance the building of a monument dedicated to Kauffman. The monument honoring a U.S. serviceman killed in action, would become one of the first in the United States to be built with public funds…. Temple would dedicate the monument at the site of the original San Gabriel Mission, where it was later moved to its present site in Temple City Park, next to City Hall…. Temple's Family participated in the ceremony, especially his young sons who were cadets at the Pasadena Army and Navy Academy …. _**World War II**_… General George Smith Patton, Jr. was born in San Gabriel in 1885, and was the leading U.S. Army general in World War II. He led campaigns in North Africa, Sicily, France, and Germany. He commanded the Third Army in the war against Germany , and was a strong advocate of armored warfare. Known as 'Old Blood and Guts' and a tough disciplinarian, his men also knew being under his command was their best chance for returning home alive. … During the Mexican Expedition of 1916, Patton served under General Pershing, and was active in the pursuit of Pancho Villa. During his service, he led his company in tracking down General Julio Cardenas, commander of Villas' personal security guard … For his action and because of his fondness for the Colt Peacemaker, Pershing gave him the nickname of 'Bandito'…. Patton died on December 21, 1945 of an embolism, after being paralyzed in an auto accident two weeks before... Patton's family plot is located in the San Gabriel Cemetery, next to the Episcopal Church of Our Savior, where Patton was baptized and confirmed….Patton's parents and grandparents are buried in the plot and a marker dedicated to Patton, provides the following, 'George S. Patton Jr. - Buried with his men of the U.S. Third Army, Hamm, Luxembourg'…. A life-size bronze statue of 'The Liberator' General George S. Patton is erected not far from the family cemetery plot….A stained glass window with scenes from Patton's' career, including a image of him riding on a tank, are located in the church... ***World War II*** …. Reyner Aguirre, was born July 30, 1918, in San Gabriel. He lived with his family in the *barrio* of San Gabriel, attended Lincoln School and graduated from Alhambra High School in 1938… He enlisted in the Navy on May 20, 1941 and was sent to San Diego for training, where he was assigned to the U.S.S. Arizona… He was on-board when Pearl Harbor was attacked on December 7, 1941. It took only one bomb to sink the Arizona, 13 minutes after the attack started. It is believed that a 1,760 pound bomb penetrated the deck of the Arizona and struck the ammunition and gunpowder magazine. The resulting explosion was devastating, sending a large cloud of smoke 800 feet into the air… By the time the Arizona had sunk, 1,177 of the 1,514 servicemen were dead, with more than 900 sailors and marines, including Aguirre, still entombed in the remains of the ship… Aguirre was awarded the Purple Heart and his name is engraved on the U.S.S. Arizona Memorial at Pearl Harbor… In 1946, the American Legion accepted the application for Reyner Aguirre Post 748 which was initiated by his many friends and fellow World War II Veterans from San Gabriel… ***World War II*** … James Darrell Landes, PFC1, 1st Tank Battalion, Marine Division, born June 12, 1932 and died April 18, 1950. He was 18 years old when he died…. Jackson G. Armstrong, Major U.S. Army Air Forces, WW II, born Aug. 31, 1919, died October 2, 2002… Both are buried in San Gabriel Cemetery…. ***Family Veterans***… I would like to mention the names of the veterans of my family, all of which we are all very proud of and should be recognized for their service to our country ….. Army - Bob Alderete (Rosemead), Army - Jim Alderete (Temple City), Army -

Jesse Alvarado (San Gabriel), Navy - Anthony Castillo (Temple City), Army – Joe R. Castillo (San Gabriel), Army - Manuel Castillo (San Gabriel), Air Force - Richard Castillo (Glendora), Army - Tony Enriquez (San Gabriel), Army - Arnulfo Murrieta (San Gabriel), Army - Robert Seiler (San Gabriel), Army - Craig Seiler Sr.(San Gabriel) and Army - Craig Seiler, Jr. (San Gabriel) who is presently serving in Iraq with the U.S. Army …. ***Noteworthy*** … Tony Enriquez was with the U.S. Army, 84th Division at the Battle of the Bulge, which lasted from December 16, 1944 to January 28, 1945. It was the largest land battle the United States was involved in with over a million men drawn into the fighting. As Uncle Tony recalls, 'it was the most god-awful weather to be in…' ***Final Quote …*** *'I will not mourn those who have died here, but honor those who have lived with honor'* … General George S. Patton, Jr., Army of the United States….

Chapter 4:   'Time Jockey' – Last At Bats – By Joe Castillo (11/19/07)

Saving Savannah – Part II .... Halloween Oktoberfest, the community fund raising event to save the Savannah Memorial Cemetery appeared to be a financial success. I'm not sure of the final accounting and how many people attended but this much I am certain of, more people are aware of the cemetery than before.... Hats off to the City of Rosemead, the El Monte Cemetery Association, especially President Randy Wiggins, the Moose Lodge, local businesses and the many volunteers who helped put on the informative, fun and entertaining event... The El Monte Cemetery Association gave free tours of the cemetery and explained the historical significance of the cemetery as well as the importance of the people who are buried there. Very knowledgeable tour guides provided the historical information with interesting side stories of twenty well-marked gravesites.... As with any historical site, there are interesting stories and Savannah is no exception. Here are my favorites...... As mentioned in my last column, Wiley R. Wilson, born in 1800 and died in 1878, served as a drummer at the age of 12 in the War of 1812 against the British. His marker indicates that he was born in Tennessee with the same birth date and death date of August 12th. His family has indicated that this is incorrect and he actually passed away in November 1878. However, the fact that he was a soldier at the age of 12 is enough to show he was one brave musician.... One of the original signers of the Constitution of the State of California, Asa Ellis is buried at Savannah. Ellis (1817 – 1890) was a County Supervisor, State Assemblyman and County Tax Collector... Perhaps one of the first in-ground mausoleums in Southern California is located within Savannah Cemetery. Internment markers are numbered and clearly identified within a burial plot... A number of Confederate soldiers are buried at Savannah, whose name may have originated from its southern roots. A savannah is a dry, tree-less area which is usually found in warmer climates, such as the south. The Savannah River, defining the border between South Carolina and Georgia, empties into the Atlantic Ocean at the port city of Savannah. ... Robert Miles Murray,

1926 – 2007, was a Los Angeles County Firefighter. He had no family when he died and L.A. County Firefighters took on the responsibility of making funeral arrangements and planning his burial. Savannah Cemetery adjacent to L.A. County Fire Station No. 42 was chosen as the burial site. Working with the firefighters, the El Monte Cemetery Association waived the cost of the burial site and L.A. County Firefighters proceeded to give Murray a special ceremonial tribute. Murray's casket was carried in a horse-drawn carriage while firefighters and fire trucks lined Valley Blvd. in a farewell salute to one of their own. ... Early pioneers of El Monte and Rosemead are buried here. The family plots of Guess, Cleminson, Steele, Slack, Durfee and Tyler are all located on the grounds.... The King Brothers, leaders of the Monte Boys, are all buried side by side. The Monte Boys were a vigilante group, which provided its own law and order to an untamed El Monte population... The Honorable Charles E. Wiggins, U.S. Congressman 1967 – 1978, former mayor and judge has a marker located within his family plot indicating he is actually buried at Arlington National Cemetery near Washington D.C.. His final encryption says *'His heart will always remain in El Monte.'* ... Grave markers of two young Japanese boys and two members of the Tokushige Family are buried in the same vicinity. Even though Japanese, the grave stones are written with Chinese characters as a show of reverence and respect associated with the language. Flowers are placed on the Tokushige Family plot more than any other plot in the cemetery... A great deal of work and repair is needed at the cemetery; some markers have been broken by tree roots or by age. The fundraising will definitely help but it is up to us to help keep it preserved for this and future generations.... ***The Huntington World***... The Huntington: Library, Art Collections, and Botanical Gardens in San Marino are just marvelous and amazing. The home of Henry E. Huntington and his wife Arabella, the Huntington contains some of the worlds and America's greatest art, manuscripts, book collections, and botanical gardens... The Art Galleries contain paintings, sculptures, statues, silverware and dinnerware of the highest quality and greatest craftsmen. The most comprehensive collection in this country of 18th and 19th century

British and French art is on display, including Thomas Gainsborough's *'The Blue Boy'* (1770) and Sir Thomas Lawrence's *'Pinkie'* (1794)… The Library's collection of rare manuscripts and books in the field of American and British History and Literature is vast with approximately 6 millions items. Among the treasures are details from Ellesmere Manuscript of Geoffrey Chaucer's The *Canterbury Tales*, circa 1410, the Gutenberg Bible (1455), Audubon's *Birds of America* and a world-class collection of Shakespeare's early works… The Botanical Gardens covers 120 acres of the Huntington grounds and includes greenhouses, plants of numerous varieties, and interactive exhibits. One of the more interesting collections is the Rose Garden, which shows the 2,000 year history of the rose… Founded in 1919, The Huntington is a private, non-profit collections-based research and educational institution. Henry Huntington was a man with vision, who had a special interest in books, art and gardens. His vision and interests led to the establishment of the Huntington as a center dedicated to research, education and beauty… Much of the collection has a value beyond comprehension and the number of security staff, installations and devices are a subtle reminder of their value and importance…. The proximity of The Huntington in the San Gabriel Valley allows us all to take advantage of this unique and special institution, and should be a must-see of places to visit…. ***Batting Cage Farewell***… The Temple City Batting Cages, long a regular retreat for baseball and softball players alike, is going to be torn down for a new commercial development. Over 30 years old, the cages have served as a development facility for little leaguers, high school and college players, as well as adults getting a little fun and exercise… The old style, arm generating pitching machines were from the 60's era and the names of Hall-of-Fame pitching greats were assigned to each cage. Batters came from all over the San Gabriel Valley to hit off the Koufax, Drysdale and Ryan machines. It is even rumored that Larry Sherry of the Dodgers gave pitching lessons there… Perhaps more than any other place in Temple City, the TC Batting Cages may have been the most popular site in the entire city… ***Holy Cow!*** …. The Mission San Gabriel has been the center of the San Gabriel Valley for over 200 years. Mission lands were used to grow crops, cultivate vineyards and raise cattle among other things. The huge number of cattle on Mission lands determined the significance and importance of the Mission itself. It is estimated that 12,000 head of cattle roamed on Mission land, which extended from San Gabriel all the way to Riverside, over 50 miles in total!... ***Opening Day...*** Santa Anita Park opened on Christmas Day, December 25th, 1934, with 30,777 patrons in attendance. Total wagers for the day accounted for $258,961, averaging just under $8.50 in wagers placed per person. Santa Anita will start its winter season on December 26th, as traditional on the day after Christmas, 73 years after its initial opening.... ***A Place Called Anita***... The name of Santa Anita has an interesting history. Many of the early Spanish places and ranchos were named after religious persons and references. The Spanish translation is 'Saint Annie', however there is no Saint Annie, and the name is more likely a diminutive of the place name Santa Ana (Saint Anne)... The name was first applied to the land in 1806 by Mission San Gabriel padres, and thereafter became known as Rancho Santa Anita. It is listed subsequently as that on five separate titles or claims to the land... The land grants of Rancho Santa Anita did not include the mountain foothills. According to the United States Forest Service (USFS), the canyon north of Rancho Santa Anita was named by E.J. 'Lucky' Baldwin, for his daughter Anita. The name was then applied to the creek which flows down it, the road running through the canyon and the street it later turns into ... As a result, Santa Anita Canyon, Santa Anita Creek, Santa Anita Canyon Road and Santa Anita Avenue were named after daughter Anita Baldwin and Rancho Santa Anita which includes the lands of present day Arcadia, Pasadena, Monrovia and Temple City, was named by the padres of the Mission San Gabriel, in honor of Saint Anne, who was the mother of the Virgin Mary. ***Nicknames***... Some the best nicknames of jockeys who have rode at Santa Anita Racetrack include 'The Shoe' (Bill Shoemaker), 'The Pirate' (Laffit Pincay) and my favorite 'Howdy Doody' (Chris McCarron).... ***Nicknames II*** ... A small local newspaper published for, by and about the Mexican-American people from the San Gabriel *barrio* was distributed in the late 1940's. It was named *'El Chismoso'* (The Tattler) and provided a surplus of information on the families and people in the local neighborhoods…. ***Street Names***… Present day Las Tunas Dr. runs east-west from Arcadia, through Temple City and San Gabriel, ending at the border with Alhambra. Walter P. Temple named the street in his design of the Town of Temple, which turned into San Gabriel Ave. at the San Gabriel city limits. Years later, it too was changed to Las Tunas Dr… ***Places To Visit…*** The Huntington Library, Art Gallery and Botanical Gardens, 1151 Oxford Rd, San Marino, CA 91108, (north entrance at Orlando Rd at Allen Ave.) Phone: 626-405-2100, Hrs: Tuesday – Friday: Noon – 4:30 PM, Saturday and Sunday 10:30 AM – 4:30 PM, Closed Mondays and major holidays. Admission: Members: FREE Non-Members: Adults - ($15), Seniors – 65 + ($12), Students - $10, Youth -age 5-11 ($6), Under 5 – FREE… Exhibits and special presentations are scheduled throughout the year. The Huntington Residence is currently being restored and the art, book and manuscript collections may be the best in the United States and on the West Coast, and are definitely the best in the San Gabriel Valley. For more information see the San Marino section in the Calendar section of the San Gabriel Valley Weekly for scheduling of upcoming events at the Huntington… ***Comments*** … Please feel free to contact me at joeacastillo@aol.com with your comments or suggestions. I look forward to hearing from you…***Noteworthy*** … Congratulations to the Temple City High School Marching Band and Pageantry Corps who won 1st Place in the prestigious La Palma Parade and Band Review…. ***Final* *Quotes***: *"I can not live without books"* – Thomas Jefferson

Chapter 5:   'Time Jockey' – *Valley of the Archangels* – By Joe Castillo (11/27/07)

 San Miguel Valley .... In 1769, the Portola Expedition, riding north from San Diego discovered our present day valley of San Gabriel. However, the valley was not named after San Gabriel (Saint Gabriel) the Archangel, but after the other Archangel, San Miguel (Saint Michael). When the Mission was founded in 1771, it was named after San Gabriel (Saint Gabriel). The full Spanish name of the Mission was '*Mision del Santo San Gabriel Arcangel de los Temblores'* (Mission of the Holy Saint Gabriel of the Earthquakes). It is thought that the expedition experienced the effects of an earthquake or two as it made its way north through present day Santa Ana while following the Santa Ana River. The name stuck when the site was moved north in 1776, especially when the padres of the Mission started to educate the natives to their religion and ways. The padres, with help from the local natives, began to grow crops, cultivate the land and raise livestock. Over the upcoming decades, the Mission grew in significance and importance to the commerce, trade and settlers of Southern California. And in time, the name San Gabriel was applied throughout the area including the San Gabriel Valley, City of San Gabriel, San Gabriel Mountains, San Gabriel Peak, San Gabriel Wilderness, San Gabriel River, San Gabriel River Freeway, San Gabriel Boulevard, San Gabriel High School, San Gabriel Handicap and you get the point.... I looked at a current street map of the San Gabriel Valley and there were 11 road references with San Gabriel and numerous geographical resources. But what happened to the name of San Miguel? Well according to the same map, there are only 3 streets named San Miguel in the San Gabriel Valley, in Arcadia, Pasadena and Walnut, and no geographical references could be identified. The name of San Miguel, even though the original name of our valley, has become little more than a footnote in our history....*Higher Education Pranks .....* The California Institute of Technology, otherwise known as Caltech, is an educational institution for the most brightest and talented students in the United States. Many of its teachers, alumni and students are world leaders in chemistry, physics, geology and technology. But from time to time, the students have enjoyed the lighter moments in life. Take for instance, the taking of class pictures in the 1920's. As was customary, all classes, freshmen, sophomores, juniors and seniors, were scheduled to take a class picture on a scheduled day. The location was usually in front of Throop Hall at 1:00 PM on a given day. The frosh class was to go first, and even though skeptical, they lined up according to height in four rows, while the students in other classes, anxiously watched while appearing to wait for their turn at taking their class photo. The photographer organized the group and took the first picture, made some adjustments, then followed with the second take and finally started counting down to take the third picture. After the third shot was taken, the plot was launched. The windows in Throop Hall overlooking the picture site flew open and students emptied wastebaskets filled with water on the unsuspecting freshmen. Not to be left out, other students would bring some other type of water hose or pump to further soak those freshmen who weren't quite wet enough....***From the Archives--- > Aged Ads ....*** This advertisement came from a 1951 publication: ' *The House of Fun - Complete line of hobby supplies – Airplanes – Boats - HO trains - Model craft supplies - Joker novelties - Figurine paintings and Free instructions. 9677 ½ E. Las Tunas Dr., Temple City, Atlantic 6-0844'* .... What, no video games, IPODs, X-BOX or PS3 ??? Also in the same publication was an ad for the San Gabriel Nursery, which at least since the late 1940's has been a generous employer of numerous people, especially local workers who found the close proximity to their home neighborhoods very beneficial....***Santa Anita Park Scribbles ....***Santa Anita Park opened on Christmas Day, 1934, with the $5,000 Christmas Stakes highlighting the inaugural racing program. High Glee, a 3-year old filly ridden by Jockey Silvio Coucci, won the race by 2 lengths and paid $14.60 to patrons with the winning ticket. But the fans were most happy when place and show money on the second place finisher, Chictoney, were shown on the board. Chictoney paid $39.00 to place and $13.40 to show, which isn't a large amount of money but based on the handle that day, the total amount of wagers placed per bettor, was only $8.48

... for the entire day! Ticket holders went home very happy having received an unexpected Christmas gift compliments of Chictoney.... **_Nicknames ...._** The Avocado, also known as the 'Alligator Pear', was a commercial fruit cultivated in the 1890's and is a native of Mexico and South America. The commercial success of the avocado grew through the turn of the century and by the 1940's large avocado groves were flourishing throughout the Puente Hills area. It all ended as suburbia expanded and housing developments sprouted where avocado groves once stood.... **_People Portfolio ...._** Jean Vignes, a planter in early Los Angeles, brought the first orange tree and planted it in Los Angeles. He brought the tree from the healthy orchards of the Mission San Gabriel, which would eventually grow throughout the San Gabriel Valley.... **_Street Guide ...._** Plans for the '10' Freeway were approved on August 7, 1947. The freeway passes through 4 western states: California, Arizona, New Mexico and Texas, with 242 miles of highway located in California. The freeway opened in 1954 between Kellogg Hill and Archibald Ave in Ontario. It was originally named Ramona Freeway, then San Bernardino Freeway and now the '10' Freeway.... **_Places to Visit ...._** The El Monte Historical Association Museum has over 8,500 square feet filled with early El Monte and San Gabriel Valley history. It is well planned with artifacts clearly and interestingly defined. My favorite item was the 1934 Rolls Royce used during World War II by President Franklin Roosevelt and Prime Minister Winston Churchill. The complete vehicle sits in the museum as the centerpiece of the war era display. Plan to spend a couple of hours viewing all displays, and it is truly one of the best and more interesting museums in the San Gabriel Valley. The museum is located at 3150 N. Tyler Ave., El Monte, 91732. Hours are Tuesday – Friday 10:00 AM – 4:00 PM and Sunday 1:00 – 3:00 PM. Call (626) 443-3813 for more information....**_Comments ...._** Please email me any comments or suggestions to joeacastillo@aol.com. If you have an interesting historical story, send it along and we'll be glad to share with our readers in a future column.... **_Noteworthy...._** Congratulations to the Los Angeles Dodgers for coming up with the brilliant idea of playing an exhibition game in the Los Angeles Memorial Coliseum, the home of the Dodgers from 1957 – 1961, while Dodger Stadium was being built.... ***Final Quotes...*** *'There is many a boy here today who looks on war as all glory, but boys it is all hell'* --- General William Tecumseh Sherman...

Chapter 6:   'Time Jockey' – *Tournament Days*   – By Joe Castillo (12/14/07)

Tournament Park …. In the early days of the Rose Parade, Tournament Park was the terminus of the parade, as well as the center of New Year's Day festivities in Pasadena. Chariot races and football games were scheduled at the park, which provided the perfect facility with picnic tables, benches, restrooms and fields of grass for games and athletics events. But the park was also the site of many first-time events. In 1911, Cal Rodgers completed the first transcontinental flight when he landed in Tournament Park. On December 10, 1910, Charles Williard was the first person to fly over Pasadena, from Tournament Park to the Arroyo Seco and back to Tournament Park. Coincidentally, the plane was built by Williard himself. In 1920, the great Charles Paddock became the 'World's Fastest Human', when he set a world's record in the 100 meter dash. The City of Pasadena decided to build a world-class Olympic track for their own star sprinter Paddock, and it was to be included within Tournament Park, which later was dedicated as Paddock Field. In one of the greatest track and field feats of all time, Paddock would go on to set six world records on the field, at distances of 90, 110, 130, 150 yards, 100 and 200 meters, all on June 18, 1921….
The Association… Beginning in 1890, the first six annual Rose Parades were held, and were organized by the Valley Hunt Club, which continues to place an entry in the annual parade. The parade originally started as a family–based event but as it grew in popularity and size, the Tournament of Roses Association was formed to handle the increased success. Parade spectators continued to celebrate New Year's Day with bicycle races, running contests, tug-of-wars, "rings", polo games and even horse racing. An available field was necessary to hold the events, and the site south of Caltech was selected. In 1901, the Association purchased the property for $6,300 and named it Tournament Park…. *Football Arrives …* The attraction of a major college football game as the center of the New Year's Day festivities, continued to gain more and more interest. In 1902, the Michigan football team was invited to play in the first Pasadena game. Michigan was a winner of 10

straight games, having outscored opponents by a 501 – 0 margin. Stanford, the best of a weak collection of Pacific Coast schools, agreed to play the mighty Wolverines. Tickets were priced from 50 cents to $1, but the Association was concerned that *'no one will pay that kind of money to see a football game'*. The field had seating for 2,500 fans but somehow 8,000 people found their way in to see the game. The oversized crowd created what many call *'the worst traffic jam in Pasadena history'*. Scheduled to start at 2:00 PM, it didn't start until 3:30, when the crowd and traffic delayed the start of the game. The first New Year's Day game was a stinker with Michigan winning 49-0, but Stanford was satisfied that it 'held' its opponent under its average of 51 points. The next year Michigan still dominated but this time no West Coast team was up for the challenge. For the next 13 years, no football game was played on New Year's Day in Pasadena.... ***The Tournament ….*** Without football, a new exciting event was needed. Polo was selected in 1904, and a group of Navajo Indians excited the crowd by participating in the parade, setting up camp and inviting the crowd in for their ceremonies. Following the popularity of 'Ben Hur', Chariot Races provided the entertainment for the next five years. But Chariot Races could sometimes become wild and unrestrained, such as when the finishers arrived together at the finish line and kept going and going until someone came out in first. The Chariot Races started to lose popularity in 1913, after being deemed too hazardous and endangering to spectators. Other events such as an ostrich race, elephant vs camel races and other exotic events became the main attraction of New Year's Day, but it was football that everyone still wanted. On January 1, 1916, the 2nd football game on New Year's Day in Pasadena was played at Tournament Park. Even though the event loss $11,000, the popularity of the event was enough to start a regular schedule of games on New Year's Day. ...***Change of Venue ...*** W.L. Leishman, Tournament of Roses Association President in 1920 and 1921, realized that the game would eventually become too big for Tournament Park, and proposed that the Arroyo Seco be used to build a larger stadium. The Arroyo was undeveloped and still wild, but provided the largest area necessary to construct a stadium to meet the growing popularity of the game. Leishman was correct in foreseeing the growth of the game. In 1921, Ohio State played California in front of the sell-out crowd at Tournament Park. Tickets sold for 65 cents each and all 30,000 seats were sold with 41,500 fans actually showing up for the game. Cal won 28-0. In 1922, Cal returned to play Washington and Jefferson College. Despite a constant rain, 40,000 fans showed up for 0-0 deadlock game. The Rose Bowl was under construction, and the 1922 game would be the last New Year's Day game played at Tournament Park. It also marked the last time festivities and events were held at the park. The parade route had been extended to Sierra Madre Blvd., and the floats would no longer be parked at Tournament Park for post-parade viewing. Shortly thereafter, the Tournament of Roses Association sold Tournament Park to Caltech, where it was to be used for sporting competitions and athletic events…. ***Game of the Century ….*** Fast forward to November 4, 1979; the Rose Bowl was host for a classic match between two teams not exactly known for their football, California Institute of Technology VS Tijuana Institute of Technology. According to a newspaper article covering the game, it was the second game of the series; Caltech won the first game by a score of 17-6. A large crowd of 200 fans was expected, but more significantly the game was a chance to be the first played in front of more than 100,000 empty seats. The Caltech team came out to exercise before the game but Tijuana Tech was nowhere to be found. The previous year, Tijuana was detained at the border for two hours but arrived in an old green bus, with plenty of time to spare. The bus barely survived the long trip, and the driver worked on it during the entire game for the return trip to Tijuana. In 1979, the Beavers of Caltech started the season with 26 players but due to injuries they were down to 18 for the Tijuana game. Due to the dwindling number of players, the team was forced to cancel its final two games of the season, making the Tijuana game their last chance to improve on their 1-5 record. At 2PM, the Caltech band arrived at the Rose Bowl. At 2:05, the card section, 7-members strong, held up cards spelling out BEAT T.I.T. (Tijuana Institute of

Technology). At 2:15, the Gorilla arrived. The Beavers are Caltech's nickname but it was believed that no more Beaver suits were available to rent so the Gorilla costume was selected Tijuana was still a no-show at game time, and even an hour later there was still no signs of Tijuana Tech. Finally the game was cancelled, that old green bus had probably made its last trip. The Caltech VS Tijuana Tech rivalry ended on a broken transmission…. ***Final Quotes*** … *'Let's score some points before they get here!'* Anonymous fan at the Caltech VS Tijuana Tech football game at the Rose Bowl.

Chapter 7: 'Time Jockey' – *Free Land* – By Joe Castillo (01-05-08)

Early Rancho Santa Anita .... The early years of the Mission San Gabriel were focused on making the mission as self-sustaining as possible, which was the objective for all the California missions. The mission was in essence a large ranch complete with orchards, irrigation, livestock and industries. According to California chronicler Alfred Robinson, two ranches or *ranchos* were established within San Gabriel Mission lands to support the self-sustaining philosophy of the mission..... Rancho San Bernardino, on the eastern border, was established for domesticated cattle and was used to feed the Mission padres and Indian laborers. Rancho Santa Anita, located 5 miles northeast of the mission, was established for cultivation purposes, to provide food stock and grain for man and animals alike.... The Mission dominated the area with its vast acreage and its free Indian labor but the Mexican revolt against the Spanish in 1821 would end their domination forever.... Without the military protection, monetary funding and overall support of the government, the Mission was left to sustain on its own. In 1833, the Mexican government ordered the secularization of all California Missions. Control of the vast Mission lands were taken away from the Mission clergy [clergy?] and given to the rancheros, who had pledged their loyalty to the new Mexican government... Rancho Santa Anita became virtually free and available to anyone willing to follow the requirements for obtaining land. All a person needed to do was promise to obey the laws of Mexico, embrace the Catholic religion and perhaps get the favor of a local official... Imagine the lands of Arcadia, San Marino, Temple City, Monrovia and eastern Pasadena all free and available. Over the next 165 years, the lands of Rancho Santa Anita escalated in value to the point where today they are the most expensive and valued in the entire San Gabriel Valley ..... ***From the Archives...
Mission Memos ....*** A previous column of the 'Time Jockey' introduced the Archangels Michael and Gabriel. So what is an archangel? It is an angel of a higher order, a higher level than a regular angel... The bible identified seven archangels: Raphael,

Uriel, Raguel, Sariel, Remiel, Michael and Gabriel. Gabriel is mentioned in the Bible as the angel who can forsee the future, and is the Angel who tells the Virgin Mary of her impending birth of Jesus Christ. Michael is the combative archangel, the angel who confronts and battles evil and I who fights the Devil for the soul of Moses... I haven't quite identified the reason why the mission was named Gabriel and the valley named Miguel (Spanish for Michael) but I have a theory on that.... San Gabriel was perhaps seen as the future center of the southern route thus providing the greatest potential for growth. San Miguel was seen as the protector of the lands and people of the mission. It's only a theory but the early Spanish explorers and padres were deeply religious and named places in honor of saints and holy events. The Mission San Gabriel was the fourth mission established, after San Diego, San Antonio and Soledad, and was the first established inland and away from the coast. If the California Missions were to survive, then the location and success of the Mission San Gabriel would be the key between the north and south, and the mission would need the protection of San Miguel... And let's not forget the earthquakes which probably scared everyone in those early years....***Nicknames***

.... 'Lucky' Baldwin, the man who developed Rancho Santa Anita into its most profitable and lucrative period of operation, received his nickname from a number of successful entrepreneur ventures... One of the earliest took place at the age of 12 when Elias Jackson (E.J.) Baldwin accepted his father's offer to drive his herd of hogs on a four-week drive to Cincinnati for slaughter. The elder Baldwin established a sale weight of 160 pounds for each hog, and agreed to pay his son for the excess weight of any hog over 160... Using his great knack for getting the most out of his investment, E.J. drove the hogs to the outskirts of Cincinnati. Two days before going to the slaughter house, E.J. bought some rather large bags of salt and spread it rather judiciously on the grains used to feed the hogs. The next day, E.J. led the hog herd to water, where the hogs drank and drank to quench their thirst caused by the salt... With swollen stomachs, E.J. took the hogs to slaughter, where the 160 pound weight was easily surpassed by a number of the bloated hogs... E.J.

netted $32 for the excess weight and used the money to buys gifts for his family, a new rifle and a horse. In three months, he sold the horse for 100% profit, and the rest is history. Baldwin was more than '*lucky*', he was also a very smart man....***People Portfolio ....*** The city of Duarte was named after Antonio Duarte, a Mexican military officer, who was assigned to protect the area around the Mission San Gabriel from the marauding Indians. Antonio Duarte established an outpost around the present day city of Duarte, and with a small number of men, kept the Indians under control.... In gratitude, the Mexican Governor granted Duarte over 4,000 acres, which he settled in the 1840's. With its rich soil and abundance of water, Duarte was able to grow excellent quality crops on his rancho. The name of 'Duarte' was stamped on crates filled with the best tasting produce of the valley and became synonymous with a quality product, even in the many years after Rancho Duarte had been sold to other owners.... ***Streets Guide ....*** Stoneman Avenue in Alhambra was probably named after General George Stoneman, who was born on August 8, 1822 in Busti, New York. Stoneman was a graduate of West Point and served under General George McClelland with the Union Army during the Civil War... Stoneman would eventually settle in the San Gabriel Valley and would go on and become Governor of California in 1882... ***Comments ....*** Please email me any comments or suggestions to joeacastillo@aol.com. If you have an interesting historical story, send it along and we'll be glad to share it with our readers in a future column....***Final Quotes...***'*They made us many promises, more than I can remember, but they never kept but one; they promised to take our land, and they took it*', Red Cloud, Oglala Dakotas Indian Chief..

A New Owner Arrives .... Following the secularization of Mission
lands, Rancho Santa Anita was virtually ownerless and
undeveloped. The Gabrielinos had established a village on the site
and had used its vast natural resources to live off the land and
sustain their dying Indian culture. In 1839, Hugo Reid, a Scottish
immigrant, Cambridge graduate, veteran South American trader
and newly naturalized Mexican citizen and Catholic, arrived in
Southern California. He married Victoria, the daughter of the
Gabrielino chief, whose tribe had settled on the lands of Rancho
Santa Anita, and adopted her four Indian children. He became the
pioneer anthropologist who recorded the primary information on
the Gabrielino culture. Reid applied for title to Rancho Santa Anita
and was granted provisional claim to 13,319 acres, which covers
most of present day Arcadia and Sierra Madre, as well as parts of
Pasadena, San Marino and Monrovia. Reid began construction of
an abobe house built in the Los Angeles style, with a flat roof and
corridors. It still remains as one of the few adobes in the area,
located on the grounds of the Arboretum. Reid, took the name of
Don Perfecto, and began to establish a prosperous rancho. He grew
wheat, vines, fruit trees and raised horses and cattle. The cattle
stock was the foundation of the rancho economy, with its beef and
leather business. With the growing prosperity of his rancho, Reid
hoped to gain the favor of Governor Pio Pico and receive full title to
Rancho Santa Anita. Finally in 1845, Reid was granted full title to
the rancho but within two years he found his life as a ranchero
exhausting and was nearly on the brink of insolvency. He offered his
land for sale at twenty cents an acre and Reid's friend and Rancho
Azusa neighbor Harry Dalton purchased the property for $2,700.
Five years later, Reid died a humble and broken man. His beautiful,
safe and prosperous Rancho Santa Anita, once deemed the 'fairy
spot of the Valley', died a slow death, with changing owners, a
transitional economy and new claims to land ownership of Rancho
Santa Anita. *History Day ....* I recently attended the 'History Day' at
the San Gabriel Mission and found it very informative, interesting

and engaging. The mission offers a varied program with knowledgeable presenters dressed in original time-era outfits. Visitors could make twine rope in a similar way that early settlers made it from hemp or siso reeds found in local riverbeds. A blacksmith demonstrated how hinges, gates and most metal used at the Mission were made. He also noted that a blacksmith did not make horseshoes, which were made by a different person with different skills. If you ever wanted to churn butter, this was the place to do it. Following the process from the early mission days, milk was allowed to sit and become cream, where it was skimmed from the top, and the remaining was churned into butter. Sheep provided wool for clothing and textiles. One process included thinning the wool through a process called carding, which produced yarn from the constant threading. Yarn was then used for sewing and making clothes. The objective of the missions was to be as self-sustaining as possible. As shown by the presenters and activities on History Day, one could see how early mission life made use of all available natural resources. 'History Days' is held the first Saturday of the month at the San Gabriel Mission and is geared towards school age students, especially 4th graders, who are working on their Mission projects. However, anyone of any age can learn from the presentations, and the 'hands-on' activities really enforce learning of the mission's daily chores of churning and carding, making pottery and molding metal....***Helping the Community ....*** In 1946, La Casa de San Gabriel Community Center was founded by Reverend Cesar Lizarraga and his wife Angelita. Lizarraga was the pastor at the Presbyterian Church on Mission Dr. in San Gabriel in 1943 and identified a need to provide educational and social services for people in the community. Working through the Presbyterian Church, the land next to the church was purchased and a community center was built. Over 60 years later, the center has provided services to tens of thousands of people in need, from infants to the elderly. Current programs include preschool education, parent education, violence prevention, adult classes, holiday gift program, youth development and food, clothing and housing programs. The center continues to be active in the community today helping those who are in need…. ***From the Archives---Mission Memos ….*** Campo Santo Cemetery was first consecrated in 1778 and is the oldest cemetery in Los Angeles County. The walls surrounding the cemetery were reconstructed in 1940; however the foundations are all original.. One marker within the cemetery is engraved 'In Memory of Antonio – 1st Indian Buried in This Cemetery – Oct. 20, 1778 – R.I.P'…***Nicknames ….*** The 'Yankee Dons' were the early Anglo-American settlers who came into the San Gabriel Valley, were granted land or married into land ownership by agreeing to be loyal citizens of Mexico and accepting the Catholic faith. Some of the early 'Yankee Dons' were John Temple, Abel Stearns and John Groningen…. ***People Portfolio ….*** The founder of Temple City was Walter Paul Temple, Sr., who married Laura Gonzalez and had five children. In order of birth, the children were Thomas Workman Temple II (1905-1972), Alvina Mercedes Temple (1906 – 1906), Agnes Evelyn Temple (1907 – 1961), Walter P. Temple, Jr. (born 1909), and Edgar Allan Temple (1910 – 1977). Alvina died shortly after birth, leaving Agnes as the only female in the family. Neither Temple nor any of his children ever lived in the City of Temple City, but Walter designated four lots, one for each child, near the intersection of Workman Ave. and Temple Ave. (now Camellia Ave.). Agnes Ave. in Temple City is named after Agnes Temple, who was also known to her brothers as 'Ines'… ***Street Guide ….*** Camellia Ave. in Temple City was named after the city motto 'Home of the Camellias', which was suggested by Mrs. Crowley of the Temple City Women's Club. The annual city parade, the Camellia Parade, also was named after the city motto. Camellia Ave. was renamed from Temple Ave., which had been named in honor of Walter P. Temple, the city founder. Subsequently, Sunset Ave. was renamed to Temple City Blvd, as the new street to honor founder Walter P. Temple Sr. …***Final Quotes…*** '*Destruction came as a thief in the night*' – Hugo Reid on mission secularization.

Chapter 9:   'Time Jockey' – *Exploring Alta California* – By Joe Castillo (02-01-08)

In this issue of 'Time Jockey' …. The early exploration of unmapped Alta California by brave men under the directive of the Spanish government; the popularity of Americas' favorite dessert – ice cream; the new changes to the old history of Santa Anita Racetrack; and the greatest chess player from Southern California, the United States and perhaps the world... ***The Presidios ….*** The development of Alta California, as it was known under the governance of Spain, was based on military and religious objectives. The Spanish government intended to educate and convert the Native Californian Indians to its Roman Catholic religion, while also using them as a source of labor to cultivate the land and build settlements, which would later become the Missions.... The other objective of Spain was to develop a military presence in Alta California. Encroachment of foreign interests was already taking place in Northern California by traders and trappers from the East. In order to build a military presence, Spain intended to build a number of '*presidios*' or military outposts along the California coast.... In 1769, an expedition under the command of Captain Gaspar de Portola traveled from Loretto, Baja California to Monterey, Alta California, seeking locations to establish the military presidios. Four sites were selected: San Diego, Santa Barbara, Monterey and San Francisco... But the Portola expedition also accomplished another significant milestone. Members of the expedition drafted a detailed record including maps of the journey. Mountains, rivers, lakes and natural plant growth were observed and documented... In the next decade, expeditions specifically looking for sites to establish a chain of California missions followed Portola's route. As a result, the site for Mission San Gabriel and the river which flowed west from the San Gabriel Valley toward present day Los Angeles were each encountered and documented during this first historic journey to explore California.... ***Screaming for Ice Cream ….*** New Year's Day draws thousands of people to Pasadena for the annual Rose Parade and Rose Bowl Game. Known as the 'Crown City', Pasadena was also a booming center in its early days for businesses. One industry which prospered in those days was the ice cream business... Fosselman's Ice Cream, with over 20 delivery trucks, delivered ice cream to all the Pasadena, South Pasadena and Alhambra schools. The ice cream plant was located at 444 S. Fair Oaks Avenue back in the 1930's and today it still operates a store in Alhambra... Another ice cream company, the Decker Ice Cream Company, operated at the same time, in the same area on El Centro Ave. in South Pasadena. Over 200,000 gallons of ice cream were manufactured each year at the Decker plant.... And finally, Burt Baskin, opened a shop in Pasadena in 1946. This was the initial footstep in today's most popular ice cream enterprise called Baskin-Robbins Ice Cream... ***Santa Anita Park Scribbles ....*** Santa Anita Racetrack has never looked better than on Opening Day. The old tote board facing the center of the main grandstand has been upgraded and is oh-so easy to read. The paddock circle where the horses are mounted and final instructions are given is looking better than ever with its manicured grass and surrounding flowers and new wood chip walking ring. In the center, the great Seabiscuit looks real enough to come off its stand and run the mile-and-a-sixteenth... Even though the park remains much as it was in the 1940's, one change was inevitable. Self-service betting machines are being installed at all betting locations significantly reducing the number of face-to-face real tellers... But rest assured, if you want to receive your winnings in the form of cash, you'll need to get it from a real teller. I guess that tells you, when it comes to betting, there are far more losers than winners at the track.....***From the Archives....People Portfolio ....*** Father Francisco Garces, one of the early adventurers to explore Alta California, recorded his journeys through the previously unchartered lands of Alta California. From 1777 – 1778, Garces traveled with his armed Spanish soldiers from Loretto, Baja California, north to San Francisco..... Without a map or road to guide him and his expedition, Garces used natural resources as his landmarks. He identified   a major tributary of the Santa Ana River which provided an abundance of resources in its riverbeds. Garces would follow the Santa Ana River north, which eventually brought him into the San Gabriel Valley by way of the San Gabriel River...

Garces noted that the San Gabriel River was easily crossable at certain locations, and it provided travel access through its shoreline. Garces also recorded the locations of mountains, hills, valleys and fertile lands as he continued towards Mission San Gabriel where he stayed for three nights... But Garces was most complimentary of his Indian guides, which rode with the expedition from Baja California. The Indians not only performed some of manual labor but also were able to communicate with the many other Indian tribes which were encountered along the way.... Without his Indians guides, it is doubtful that Garces would have reached his destination and leave behind a record of his fact finding journey for future followers ..... ___Noteworthy ....___ Bobby Fischer, the recluse and former World Chess Champion, died last month in Iceland. Born and raised in New York, he learned to play chess at the age of 6 after his sister bought him a chess set for his birthday.... In 1956, at 13 years of age, he became the youngest person to win the United States Jr. Chess Championship. In 1958, at 16, he became the U.S. Chess Champion and was given the title of grandmaster, the youngest person ever to receive such a title. Between 1958 and 1967, Fischer won 8 of 10 U.S. Chess Championship Tournaments... With Fischers' success, the popularity of the game of chess boomed with sales of chess sets and boards taking off. In 1964, Fischer played 50 simultaneous chess games in a much publicized event in Hollywood.... Finally, in 1972, Fischer played Soviet Champion Boris Spassky for the World Championship. After forfeiting his second match and trailing 2-0 in the best-of-24 series, Fischer rallied to soundly defeat Spassky and claim the title of World Champion. He was only 29 years old. ... Three years later, Fischer forfeited his title after failing to get a rule change. In another first, he became the only person to give up the World Chess Champion title without losing a game..... In time, Fischer became more withdrawn from society and preferred to be alone. He made racially insensitive and Anti-American remarks which were received poorly from his public following. He drifted from place to place, especially around the Los Angeles and Pasadena area.... Early in my working career, I heard a rumor that Fischer visited the

Pasadena Library on Walnut Street on a regular basis and I attempted to seek out the greatest chess player in the world... After a number of visits, I gave up. Bobby Fischer was nowhere to be found, which is exactly where he wanted to be .... ***Prediction...*** Using the historical fact that no team has gone undefeated since the 1972 Miami Dolphins, I'm going with the NY Giants by a 27-24 margin in Super Bowl 42.... I remember listening to Super Bowl I on the radio, even though it was carried by two television stations. Incidentally, it wasn't called the Super Bowl back then, it was known as the 'AFL-NFL World Championship Game' .... ***Final Quotes...*** Fischer was *'a prisoner of chess who got lost in its depths and could not find his bearings in the real world outside'* – Gary Kasparov, Russian Chess grandmaster ....

Chapter 10: 'Time Jockey' – *President's Day* – By Joe Castillo (2/16/08)

In this issue of 'Time Jockey' - In honor of President's Day, we look at: President Richard Milhous Nixon; the Robert Kennedy presidential campaign; President Herbert Hoover's strong support, President Franklin D. Roosevelt campaign offices; and a Canadian, Pacific Coast explorer and his observations... ***Whittier President*** .... Richard Milhous Nixon, 37th President of the United States, was born and raised in Southern California. He was born on January 9th, 1913, in his parents' ranch home in Yorba Linda where he spent the first nine years of his life. .. Shortly thereafter, his family moved to Whittier and he attended East Whittier elementary schools, Whittier High School and Whittier College. After earning his law degree from Duke University Law School and fulfilling a tour of duty in the U.S. Navy, he met his wife, Patricia 'Pat' Ryan. The future Mrs. Nixon was a Whittier school teacher. In 1940 they were married at the Mission Inn in Riverside in front of a small gathering. Nixon had little funds to pay a photographer so no pictures of the wedding exist because none were taken. In 1946, Nixon was elected to the U.S. House of Representatives representing the 12th Congressional district in California. Four years later, he won election to the U.S. Senate representing California. In 1952, Nixon was selected by Dwight D. Eisenhower to be his vice president in the upcoming presidential elections. Nixon campaigned hard for Eisenhower in Southern California and his hard work paid off. Eisenhower was elected President and Nixon was his Vice-President for the next eight years. But Nixon's luck would turn. Nixon would lose the in the 1960 Presidential Election and in the 1962 California Gubernatorial Election. After staying out of public life for the next 5 years, Richard Nixon was called back by his loyal and enthusiastic supporters. His return proved successful and finally, in 1968, he was elected as President of the United States. While he was the President, California became the focus of the country during vacation and summer months when President Nixon made his San Clemente residence the 'summer White House.' Always seeking to be involved in local historical organizations, Nixon was a member of the Native Sons of the Golden West Ramona Parlor #109, now headquartered in San Gabriel, even while he was working in Washington. President Richard Nixon died in 1994 and was buried at his presidential library in Yorba Linda, next to his family home in which he was born eighty-one years earlier. First Lady Pat Nixon, who died in 1993, is buried beside him. ***Campaigning at the Mission ....*** 1968 was a year like no other ever experienced by this country. The country was in a state of change and people were tired of the old ways. Civil rights, women rights, war protests and peace rallies were taking place in the streets, schools and neighborhoods. 1968 was also a presidential election year and candidates were campaigning hard to be the next president to succeed President Johnson. One of those candidates was Robert Kennedy, brother of President John F. Kennedy, a former U.S. Attorney General and a U.S. Senator from New York. Kennedy had entered the presidential campaign late but was gathering a strong following. After winning a couple of earlier state primaries, Kennedy entered the California primary. The close competition among Democratic Party candidates would make California a prize worth winning.... Kennedy, seeking votes in the upcoming primary, campaigned in Southern California the week before the election. While riding in a car caravan, he shook hands with potential voters in El Monte and Monterey Park. The day before the election, Kennedy visited the San Gabriel Mission and shook hands with students from San Gabriel Mission School. On Tuesday, June 6, 1968, Senator Kennedy won the California primary by a narrow margin.... The Kennedy campaign headquarters was located at the Ambassador Hotel in Los Angeles. After Kennedy was declared the winner by national media stations, he came out and addressed his large group of supporters who had gathered in the ballroom of the Ambassador. It would be his last public appearance. Shortly after midnight, Kennedy was shot in the pantry of the ballroom kitchen... He died the next day, ending the dream he had of bringing the people of this country together and ushering in a new era of change. That was 1968 ...... ***California for Hoover .....*** In the 1928 California Presidential Primary, voters had the option of selecting any candidate of their choice. Only one

Republican Party candidate was on the ballot, Secretary of Commerce Herbert Hoover. For the Democrats, New York Governor Al Smith and U.S. Senator James Walsh of Montana were on the ballot…. The final count of Los Angeles County for the May 3rd primary was Hoover with 240,885 votes with second-place Smith registering only 37,373 votes. A majority of San Gabriel Valley towns heavily favored Hoover. San Marino with only 904 registered voters in 1928 backed Hoover by a 19 to 1 margin over Smith. Hoover tallied 1,789 votes in Monrovia while Walsh recorded only 207. In Sierra Madre, fifty percent of the registered voters turned out and backed Hoover 496 to 67. South Pasadena followed much like the other cities heavily backing Hoover. The general election in November went much like the California Primary vote. Hoover became the 31st President of the United States, winning 444 electoral votes to 87 for Al Smith. Hoover's term lasted four years when he lost re-election in 1932 to the new Governor of New York Franklin D. Roosevelt. ***El Monte Support …..*** In late 1934, after President Roosevelt announced he would seek a second term, a campaign office was opened in El Monte on Valley Boulevard. Posters of the group supporting Roosevelt stated; 'Americans Supporting Democracy – an organization of Democrats against Sinclair and Socialism'. ***Early Pioneers ….*** In 1793, British explorer George Vancouver sailed along the Southern California coast looking for the newly established pueblo of Los Angeles. He never was able to spot the settlement from the sea but he did note the abundant vegetation growth and openness of the area. Vancouver recorded the following in his journal, 'a very advantageous settlement is established on this fertile spot….the country town of the Angels'…. ***Final Quotes…*** *'Always remember others may hate you but those who hate you don't win unless you hate them. And then you destroy yourself' – Richard M. Nixon, 37th President of the United States.*

Chapter 11:   'Time Jockey' – *Fantoystic* – By Joe Castillo (02-22-08)

Flying with Wham-O .... Richard Knerr, co-founder of Wham-o, died last month at the age of 82. Knerr, along with partner Arthur 'Spud' Melin, founded the successful toy manufacturing company whose toys would be used by future generations of fun-loving kids.... Working from Knerr's garage in South Pasadena in 1948, Kneer and Melin purchased a Sears band saw and started making slingshots. They sold the slingshots through Popular Mechanics magazine and began receiving royalties on a regular basis... While firing the slingshot during its development stage, Melin would make a *'wham-o'* sound when a target was hit. The name stuck and when the company was formed Wham-O was selected as the company name.... A string of successful products soon followed including Slip 'N Slide (1961), Limbo Game (1962), Superball (1966), Silly String (1972), and Hacky Sac (1983). But it was the manufacturing of its two most successful products, the Frisbee and the Hula Hoop, which pushed Wham-O on its way to expanded operations.... In 1958, the Hula Hoop was designed after an Australian exercise device. The hoop was tested in Pasadena schools and successful hula-hoopers were allowed to keep the toy if they could keep it going around their hips... At peak popularity, 200,000 hoops were produced a day and within 4 months Wham-o claimed Hula Hoop sales of $25 million... Also in 1958, Wham-O bought the rights of the Plutto Platter from an inventor named Fred Morrison. Knerr and Melin modified the platter and renamed it the 'Frisbee'. The name was taken from the comic strip 'Mr. Frisbee' and manufacturing began immediately. In a 30-year period, over 100 million Frisbees were sold... The success of the Frisbee and Hula Hoop prompted Knerr and Melin to open new manufacturing plants in the San Gabriel Valley. One the sites was located in San Gabriel, on Gladys and El Monte Ave, one block east of San Gabriel Blvd, adjacent to the San Gabriel Nursery.... During the holiday season, Wham-O would hire a number of temporary workers to meet the increased demand to produce toy products for the upcoming holiday season. The period lasted approximately 3 months and workers were released right after the Christmas season. In my younger days, I applied for one of those temporary positions. I was hoping my vast experience playing with the toys would surely land me a coveted position. Alas, it seemed that there were a number of other applicants who had also used the toys and most of the positions were given to them. At least I still had my Air Blaster, which in my opinion was the best Wham-O toy produced …. Eventually, the company was sold in 1982 and another toy company, Mattel, acquired Wham-O in 1994. Those were sure the good ol' days….

Back to the Rancho ….When we last wrote about Rancho Santa Anita, Hugo Reid had sold his beautiful rancho to Harry Dalton of Azusa. The year was 1847 and over the next 15 years ownership of the property passed from one person to the next…. Starting in 1862, the southland experienced 3 years of heavy rainfall. The rain was good for the land but bad for livestock. Cattle and sheep died by the thousand. Ranches lost their main source of income and were forced into foreclosure. Rancho Santa Anita was no exception…. In order to raise money, the rancho was sub-divided into two parts. The western portion consisted of 2,000 acres and was sold for $2 per acre. A German merchant and entrepreneur named Leonard Rose bought the property… The remaining 11,319 acres, which included the area around the Reid adobe home site was sold to William Wolfskill for $20,000, approximately $1.75 an acre…. **_Early Inhabitants_** … The indigenous people who worked the San Gabriel Mission from 1770-1830's were given the name of Gabrielinos by the Spanish Missionaries. They were the early inhabitants of the San Gabriel Valley. By the beginning of the 20th century, the Gabrielino's were nearly extinct. Their culture, language and even the name they called themselves had all been replaced by the Spanish administrators and Mission clergy …. In 1492, when Columbus arrived in the New World, California was the most densely populated region in the future United States. There were more tribes and languages spoken here than in any other area of the same size….Fifty years later, Juan Cabrillo discovered California, with an estimated native population of 310,000. Cabrillo first visited the port of San Diego, followed by Santa Catalina and

San Clemente Islands. He had no problems with the natives and would term his encounters as 'friendly'.... Cabrillo also laid anchor outside of Santa Monica Bay but did not come ashore. Even though the natives who came out to meet him at his ship were excited and animated, they were non-threatening. ... Cabrillo had arrived during the hunting season, and from his view off the coast, he saw the smoke of a large number of camp fires. The coast of present day Long Beach was the heart of the Gabrielino world with 20-30 villages of 500 persons each. Cabrillo would name this area *'La Bahia de Los Fumos'* or Bay of Smokes.... Future Spanish explorers would later follow Cabrillo's route. One such exploration came in the springtime. A sailor on that voyage, viewing the San Gabriel Mountains, noticed a 'gold' line at the bottom of the mountains. They called it *'Sabanilla de Oro'* (Altar Cloth of Gold), which became Altadena's first non-native name.... The gold color came from the wild flowers growing along the foothills. The Spanish called the flower *'Copa de Oro'* (cup of gold), which was to become our state flower, the California Golden Poppy. It is also the City of Altadena's Official Flower... The Gabrielinos have long vacated the land, but the golden flower still grows in our foothills... **Comments ....** Please email any comments or suggestions to joeacastillo@aol.com. If you have an interesting historical story, send it along and we'll be glad to share it with our readers in a future column... ***Final Quotes...*** *"The coroner's jury sat on the body of a dead Indian. The verdict was 'Death of intoxication or by a visitation from God.'"*. – Notes from a Los Angeles vigilante trial....

Chapter 12: 'Time Jockey' – *Preserving Nature* – By Joe Castillo (03-07-08)

Sunnyslope …. Leonard J. Rose was one of the first persons to purchase property from the subdivided Rancho Santa Anita. His claim consisted of 2,000 acres on the western boundaries of the Rancho... Rose started to irrigate his estate, which he had named Sunnyslope, and built a Woodworth house to live in. With his land fully irrigated he began growing citrus trees and experimented with cultivating grapes. Eventually, Rose established one of the first vineyards in the area. His interest in agriculture was great and for many years he sought to establish an agricultural park in Los Angeles. But his main interest was raising prize trotters. The Rose stable became widely known throughout Southern California. Great champion horses such as Stromboli, Moor, and Beautiful Belle were included in his stable.... With a growing stable of horses, Rose used his Rose Meade Ranch to raise his prize racing horses. He eventually shifted from trotters to thoroughbreds, and in the process created competition with 'Lucky' Baldwin's stable.... In the early years of their rivalry, Baldwin dominated the competition. And like most horse owners of that time, they tended to bet heavily on their own horse. Baldwin was no exception and won some significant wagers in those early years..... However, Rose continued to raise horses and unlike Baldwin, he chose to sell a horse after it had won a race or was in peak form. Rose's stable was always in a state of flux, with his race horses young and fresh.... Baldwin used an opposite approach and would keep and race a horse well after his better days were behind him. According to one observer and probable bettor, when a Rose-owned horse competed against a Baldwin-owned horse, most of the time Rose came out on top... Rose's winnings increased while Baldwin suffered heavy losses betting on his own older and oft-time slower horses.... ***Don Juan ….*** The Temple Family has long been a staple of San Gabriel Valley History. The first Temple Family member to come to Southern California was Jonathan (John) Temple.... Temple arrived in California in 1827 from Boston, Massachusetts, where he had become a successful and wealthy cattleman. Temple settled in Los Angeles, and opened up a small store providing ranch, livestock and housing supplies. The site was located at the present day location of the Federal Building(in Los Angeles). His timing was excellent and his business started to gain increases in sales. With his success, Temple began to expand his business operations. He built the first market in Los Angeles, at the present day site of City Hall and the courthouse. Temple Block, one of the first two-story buildings in the young town, became the first office building in the city. Its size was relative to a city block. He and his brother constructed the building with a wooden boardwalk around the entire building. This allowed people coming off the dirty and muddy streets, to knock off some of the dirt before entering the Temple building, as well as preparing those leaving the building. The street was eventually paved and is now known as Temple St. in Los Angeles …. Temple converted to the Mexican culture becoming a Mexican citizen and Catholic Church member. He married Rafaela Coto of a long-standing and wealthy Mexican family. Temple becomes known as *'Don Juan'*, one of the new 'Yankee Dons'…. Through his marriage, he is granted possession of Rancho Los Cerritos, covering parts of present day Long Beach… Jonathan 'Don Juan' Temple was the first member of the enterprising Temple Family to come to Southern California. He was the oldest in the family and eventually his youngest brother, Pliny Fisk Temple, came west to visit his brother John in 1841. Pliny Fisk Temple would eventually have a son, Walter P. Temple, who would become founder of Temple City…. ***Azusa Recollections …..*** While doing research in a local museum, I came across a letter written in 1982 about the early days of the Azusa area. According to Winifred S. Blatchley, his grandfather, William S. Hanes, was born in Germany in 1852 and immigrated to the U.S. in 1875. He came to California and settled in Azusa, where he eventually died in 1920…. Hanes bought land on the Gladstone development, between present day Azusa and Pasadena. He chose this particular plot because of the good stand of cactus, which meant good water and soil. Hanes cleared the land of sage brush and cactus, and planted some of the first citrus trees in the area… With his brother J. Phillips, he opened the first merchandise store in the Upper San Gabriel Valley. The store also doubled as a bank and was the first to implement a new savings program…. For 5 cents, a youngster could purchase a stamp which was put into a stamp book for collecting 100 stamps. When the book was filled, $5 worth of stamps was included in the book. The book was eventually picked up by a Mr. Sartori of Los Angeles, who deposited the $5 into the youngsters account. Eventually Mr. Sartori would go on and start up Security First National Bank located at Main and Second Streets in Los Angeles…..***Back in Time….*** The Whittier Narrows Natural Area Park and Nature Center is located on over 400 acres in the southern portion of the San Gabriel Valley, near the westerly edge of the San Gabriel River. The name of 'Whittier Narrows' was based on the narrow gap between the Montebello Hills and the Puente Hills, which are located just to the south of the park…. It is located in a low flood basin which provides for a high water table and rich soil to support streamside plant growth. The area provided an ample supply of wild animals and was a prime hunting area for the Tongva-Gabrielino people, who had established a site just east of the park…. In 1939, the property where the nature center is now was purchased by the National Audubon Society, who operated the center for the next 30 years. Tours for school students and the public were conducted by the Audubon staff. Eventually it was designated a wildlife sanctuary… In July 1970, Los Angeles County of Parks and Recreation acquired the sanctuary and nature center, whose main goal was to educate the public on the natural environment, while preserving the park as a sanctuary and reintroducing native plant species to the area. The area is home to numerous types of wildlife, especially birds, as well as plants and trees. Much of the environment remains as it was in the days of Tongva-Gabrielinos' as well as the early Spanish explorers. It is one of the few places which have remained relatively intact while dedicated to the preservation of the native environment. The nature center displays a collection of wildlife which made the 'narrows' home. Once live reptiles, insects and raccoons offer a first hand look at Southern California wildlife which one rarely might see with the growth of homes throughout the valley…. But alas all good things don't last forever.

black so as not to be seen from the air. Robinson decided to enlist in the Army and served from 1942-44. After leaving the Army, Robinson played for the Kansas City Monarchs in the Negro Leagues, where he eventually caught the eye of the Dodgers organization and owner Branch Rickey, who personally presented a contract to Robinson to play baseball for the Dodgers…. Two years later, at the age of 28, Robinson was signed to a major league contract for the minimum amount of $5,000. In Robinson, Rickey saw a religious young man who was educated, had served his country in the military, been brought up in a racially mixed neighborhood of Pasadena and was an exceptional athlete. With these personal qualities, Rickey decided Robinson was ready to become the first black player to play in the major leagues. In 1947, Robinson started the season for the Brooklyn Dodgers and enjoyed an outstanding season to win the National League Rookie of the Year Award, the first time it was ever awarded…. He played 12 seasons with the Dodgers, including the 1955 World Championship team, and was eventually traded to the San Francisco Giants, the Dodgers hated rivals. But Robinson wanted no part of the Giants and rather than reporting he decided to retire…. Following his retirement, he became involved with several Civil Rights causes and was selected to serve on the Board of Directors of the NAACP…. In 1962, he was elected to baseball's highest level, the Hall Of Fame. But Robinson's final baseball tribute arrived 35 years later. On April 15, 1997, on the 50th Anniversary of Robinson's major league debut, Major League Baseball permanently retired his number 42. Only nine players who were wearing No. 42 at the start of the 1997 season were allowed to continue to wear it for the remainder of their careers. Today, only one player of the nine continues to wear Robinson's No. 42, New York Yankee pitcher Mariano Rivera… Throughout Pasadena, Robinson is remembered from Jackie Robinson Field at the Rose Bowl, to Jackie Robinson Park and Youth Center. His aggressive style of playing baseball were his trademark, but the composure, strength and dignity he showed while becoming the first black to play major league baseball was truly inspirational and heroic….***Mighty Matador ….*** Mike Krukow, the 'Polish Prince', was a multi-talented athlete at San Gabriel High School. He played Varsity Football, Basketball and Baseball while he attended the school from 1967-1970... As a senior, he wore jersey number 35 and was the starting catcher. ... After graduation, he attended Cal Poly San Luis Obispo, where he was converted to a pitcher. He was drafted in 1973 by the Chicago Cubs in the 8th round and on Sept. 6, 1976, he made his major league debut. ... After five average seasons, Krukow was traded to the Philadelphia Phillies, in a multi-player trade for a former rival of his from Alhambra H.S., Dan Larsen.... Following his time with the Phillies, Krukow was traded to the San Francisco Giants in another multi-player trade which included future Hall of Famer Joe Morgan.... Krukow's best seasons were with San Francisco; especially 1986 when he won 20 games for the playoff bound Giants. He finished his 12-year career with a 124 – 117 record, and continues to be a part of the San Francisco Giants organization, providing his insightful commentary as a radio and TV announcer....***Fun Games ...*** I think my love for baseball started with Little League. My first season was in 1964 in San Gabriel Eastern Little League for a team named the White Sox.... In those days, we wore old-style wool uniforms with buttoned-down jerseys. Each team was sponsored by a business, whose name was displayed on the front of each jersey. The White Sox was sponsored by Data Machines Inc. and the letters 'DMI' were sewn vertically on the front of our jerseys.... The kids of the other teams translated the 'DMI' initials to something more creative and amusing, in this case 'Dumb Monkeys Incorporated'. All year long we had to put up with the taunts and jokes, but in the end, we got even. The DMI White Sox would win the league championship two seasons in a row.... My first manager on the White Sox was George Franceschini whose son Paul played for the team. Mr. Franceschini was a fun-loving guy who made playing Little League fun, too. I recently had the pleasure of talking to Mr. Franceschini for the first time since 1965. He is 80 years old now but he still remembers that team and his players. One thing you always remember is your first Little League manager, and Mr. Franceschini made playing baseball so enjoyable and fun that he will never be forgotten... ***Keeping the***

dream alive... Ryan Tucker, Temple City HS class of 2005, 1st round draft pick of the Florida Marlins, is slated to pitch for the Marlins 'AA' Carolina Mudcats in North Carolina. Last season, Tucker finished with 133 strikeouts, the 4th highest in the Marlin Minor League organization. As a senior at TCHS, Tucker went 6-4, with a 1.13 ERA, 112 KO's in 68 innings. Tucker starred in Temple City American Little League, going 13-2 in 1999 for the Tournament of Champions District 18 Major Division Champion TCALL Tigers, which finished 24-2, winning the last 23 in a row... Eddie McKiernan, Monrovia HS class of 2007, 17th round pick of the California Angles, now pitching in the Angels minor league organization. McKiernan pitched the Wildcats to the 2006 CIF Division V Baseball title, winning CIF Division V Player of the Year honors. McKiernan was a TCALL All Star, with his Tiger teams winning District 18 Tournament of Champion titles in 1998 and 1999. He and Ryan Tucker played on the same 1999 Tiger team... Sean O'Leary, TCHS class of 2003, now pitches in the Independent Leagues in Chicago. O'Leary was the winning pitcher on the 2007 NCAA Division II Western Regional Champion Cal State Los Angeles team. In the Championship game, O'Leary pitched 8 innings in relief giving up 5 hits, 1 run, 2 walks with 2 KO's in leading the Golden Eagles to an 8-3 victory. O'Leary was a TCALL All-Star with the Angels playing shortstop and batting leadoff.... Bryce Schone, now pitches for Cal State Northridge, after two seasons at Fullerton JC. Schone played for the TCALL Angels 1997-99, and was a pitcher for the 1997 District 18 9 &10 Year Old Champion Tournament Team ... Jimmy Brittl, 39th round draft pick of the Cleveland Indians in 2006, went 3-0, with a 2.50 ERA and 20 K's in 36 innings for the Indians 'A' Mahoning Valley Scrappers last season, playing in Nile, Ohio. Brittl was a 1996 TCALL All-Star and was one of the starting pitchers for the 1st Place Major Mariners managed by Tom Chavez. The left-handed Brittl pitched at Cal State Northridge before being drafted by the Indians ... Ryan Goetz, Bishop Amat class of 2006, now plays baseball for UC Riverside. Goetz was an TCALL All-Star playing for the 1998 Major League Champion A's managed by his dad John. Goetz was also a member of the 1997 District 18 9 &10 Year Old Champion Tournament

Team... These are just some of the local players still pursuing their dream of playing professional baseball. One day, I'll be writing an article about the major league careers of these young players and they'll be the ones inspiring the next generation of San Gabriel Valley baseball players...... **_Quotes_** ... '*That isn't stealing, it's grand larceny*'.... Pasadena *Post* columnist Rube Samuelson, commenting on Jackie Robinson's base stealing ability....

Chapter 14: 'Time Jockey' – *Field of Dreams II* – By Joe Castillo (3/21/08)

Jackie Robinson …. The greatest baseball player, and perhaps athlete, from the San Gabriel Valley was Jackie Robinson. Born Jan. 31, 1919 in Cairo, Georgia, the Robinson family including five children, moved to Pasadena where they bought a home on Pepper St. The Robinson's were the first black family to live on Pepper St. and they were not well received. The Robinson children, including Jackie, endured numerous racial taunts and prejudices. But Jackie learned to stand up for himself at an early age and learned to hold his tongue when he was confronted. … Robinson attended John Muir Technical HS where he excelled in all the major sports and some minor ones. He was the top scoring, play making guard on the basketball team. He led the baseball team to the regional high school baseball championship. He won the Southern California Prep Title in the Long Jump. He won the Pacific Coast Negro Tennis Junior Tennis Tournament Championship. In football, he played quarterback, running and throwing, to lead his team to an undefeated season until the final championship game. … Robinson graduated from high school and attended Pasadena City College, where he continued to play and excel in the four major sports. He starred in the State Junior College Championship Football Game vs Compton College at the Rose Bowl, where 40,000 fans, the largest crowd to ever see a junior college football game, were in attendance…. Robinson moved on to UCLA, where be became the first 4-sport letterman in football, basketball, baseball and track. After his college eligibility expired, Robinson looked for work but could only find minimally paying positions. He went to Hawaii where he played semi-pro football and was on a ship heading home to Southern California when Pearl Harbor was attacked. Not knowing who the Japanese would attack, the ship painted their windows black so as not to be seen from the air. Robinson decided to enlist in the Army, in which he served from 1942-44. After leaving the Army, Robinson played for the Kansas City Monarchs in the Negro Leagues. He eventually caught the eye of the Dodger organization and owner Branch Rickey personally presented a contract to Robinson to play baseball for the Dodgers. Rickey sent him to the Dodgers minor league team in Montreal, the Royals. A year later in 1947, at the age of 28, Robinson was signed to a major league contract for the minimum amount of $5,000. In Robinson, Rickey saw a religious young man who was educated, had served his country in the military, been brought up in a racially mixed neighborhood of Pasadena and was an exceptional athlete. With these personal qualities, Rickey decided Robinson was ready to become the first black player to play in the major leagues. In 1947, Robinson started the season for the Brooklyn Dodgers and enjoyed an outstanding season to win the National League Rookie of the Year Award, the first time it was ever awarded. He played 12 seasons with the Dodgers, including the 1955 World Championship team, and was eventually traded to the San Francisco Giants, the Dodgers' hated rivals. But Robinson wanted no part of the Giants and rather than reporting decided to retire. Following his retirement he became involved with several Civil Rights causes and was selected to serve on the Board of Directors of the NAACP. In 1962, he was elected to the Baseball Hall Of Fame. Shortly afterwards, his uniform number 42 was permanently retired by every major league baseball team in honor of Jackie Robinson. Throughout Pasadena, Robinson is remembered: from Jackie Robinson Field next to the Rose Bowl, to Jackie Robinson Park and Youth Center. His aggressive style of playing baseball were his trademark, but the composure, strength and professionalism he showed while becoming the first black to play major league baseball was truly inspirational and heroic.... ***Little League World Series or Bust ....*** The San Gabriel Valley has always been a hot bed for young budding baseball players even from the very early days of Little League. Baseball has always had a place in our area. But for all the Little League organizations, teams and players in the San Gabriel Valley, only one team has been good enough to make the trip to the Little League World Series. In 1964, La Puente National Little League achieved the rare feat. In California, an All-Star from a local little league played in a district tournament consisting of All-Star teams from other local little leagues. Winners continued on through

Sectional, Divisional and Regional Tournaments, with the winner going on to play in the Little League World Series in Williamsport, Pennsylvania. In 1964, the tournament was single elimination and a team could only lose once before it was eliminated. The La Puente National Little League All-Star team easily won their District 20 and Section 7 Championships advancing to play in the Divisional Tournament in San Diego. Only 4 teams were in the Divisional Tournament and La Puente National drew the home team San Diego American in the first game. In a closely contested game, La Puente won by a score of 6-5 and then went on to win the Division Championship Game against San Fernando Sun Valley by a score of 5-2. It was on to the Western Regionals for La Puente National, where three other teams were also ready to play. First up for La Puente was Chico Westside representing Northern California. The game was a blowout with La Puente winning 9-1. Then in the championship game La Puente played the team from British Columbia, Trail Little League. In an exciting and competitive game, La Puente came from behind late in the game to win the decisive game 4-3 and earn a trip to the Little League World Series, becoming the first and only San Gabriel Valley team to do so....

Mighty Matador .... Mike Krukow, the 'Polish Prince', was a multi-talented athlete at San Gabriel High School. He played Varsity Football, Basketball and Baseball while attending the school from 1967-1970... As a senior, he wore jersey number 35 and was the starting catcher. ... After graduation, he attended Cal Poly San Luis Obispo, where he was converted to a pitcher. He was drafted in 1973 by the Chicago Cubs in the 8th round and on Sept. 6, 1976, he made his major league debut. ... After five average seasons, Krukow was traded to the Philadelphia Phillies, in a multi-player trade for a former rival of his from Alhambra H.S., Dan Larsen.... Following his time with the Phillies, Krukow was traded to the San Francisco Giants in another multi-player trade which included future Hall of Famer Joe Morgan. Krukow's best seasons were with San Francisco especially 1986 when he won 20 games for the playoff bound Giants. He finished his 12-year career with a 124 – 117 record, and today continues to be a part of the San Francisco Giants organization, providing his insightful commentary as a radio and TV announcer…. ***Fred Lynn* ….** In 1971, a young athlete from El Monte was making news with the Lions of El Monte. His name was Fred Lynn. On the Varsity Basketball team, he was one of the starting guards, on the Varsity Baseball team he was the starting center fielder. Lynn had an outstanding senior season batting over .400 and leading the Lions to the Mission Valley League crown. After graduating, he attended USC and played for the Trojans for two seasons before being drafted by the Boston Red Sox. He played 4 years in the minors before making his major league debut. In 1976, Lynn was the starting center fielder and batted .326, with 34 home runs and 115 RBI's. Boston would win the American League pennant and play the Cincinnati Reds in one of the greatest World Series ever played. Following the season, Lynn was awarded American League Most Valuable Player and Rookie of the Year Awards, only the second time that feat had been accomplished. Lynn would play 14 seasons with the Red Sox, Angels and Padres, before retiring. I remember watching Fred Lynn playing in an El Monte High School game his senior season. He made the plays in the field look easy but his bat was quiet for most of the day. Finally, late in game with the outcome still in doubt, Lynn delivered a hit to the gap which tied the game for the Lions. He then scored the winning run when one of the Ferguson brothers drove him in with the winning hit. Like all good players, they'll eventually come through when it is needed most and Lynn was no exception to delivering a big game winning play …. ***Larry Doby*…** Like Jackie Robinson, Larry Doby had to endure insurmountable pressures just to play baseball. He was the first black player to play in the American League, going through the same prejudices and bigotry as Robinson. On July, 5, 1947, Doby was called up to play for the Cleveland Indians. A little more than 60 days earlier, Jackie Robinson had become the first black player to play in the Major Leagues, playing second base for the Brooklyn Dodgers. Now it was Doby's turn to fill a need for the Indians and play second base. He would play 12 seasons, all in the American League for Cleveland, Chicago, Detroit and Baltimore. His best season was 1952 when he hit 32 home runs with 126 RBI's and finished second in MVP voting. He was named to 7 straight All-Star teams and finished his career with a .283 batting average, 253 HR's and 970 RBI's. In 1998, he was elected to the Baseball Hall of Fame. While attending a Dodgers vs. Pirates game on July 10, 1983 with family, we noticed a man sitting in the row ahead of us. He sported a diamond ring with a baseball field design. It was Larry Doby and when asked about the ring, he politely told us it was from the 1954 World Series and let us all take a look at it. He calmly answered our excited questions about his great career and that 1954 championship season, and then autographed our tickets. We finally let him enjoy the game, but whether the Dodgers won or lost that day, we were the real winners for having met the gentleman Larry Doby…. ***Dan Larsen ….*** Another of the outstanding Alhambra H.S. athletes was Dan Larsen. He graduated from Alhambra HS in 1972 after playing 3 years of Varsity Baseball. He played his first major league game on July 18, 1976 with the Houston Astros and later played for the Philadelphia Phillies and Chicago Cubs. His career lasted seven seasons and he finished with a 10-25 records. I remember my school, San Gabriel HS playing Alhambra HS that season in games that would decide the Mission Valley League championship. Long time rivals, the schools wasted no time in trying to intimidate each other with constant trash talking. The games were very close and competitive but Alhambra HS won both games by scores of 2-1 and 1-0. The AHS winning pitcher, who pitched two complete games, was Dan Larsen….. ***Mike McCormick…*** Mike McCormick, Alhambra HS graduate, was born on Sept. 23, 1938 in Pasadena. After being drafted by the New York Giants, he made his major league debut on Sept. 3, 1956. He played 16 seasons mostly with the Giants, and also with the Orioles and Senators. He was a 4 time All-Star playing in both All-Star games in 1960 and 1961. His best season was 1967 when he went 22-10, winning the Cy Young Award and being named The Sporting News Pitcher of the Year. Even though McCormick had a very successful career, he will always be remembered as the best National League pitcher after the retirement of Dodger Sandy Koufax and before the rise of the great Giant pitcher Juan Marichal, both future Hall of

Famers... **_San Gabriel Little League_** ... I think my love for baseball started with Little League. I first played in 1964 in San Gabriel Little League for a team named the White Sox. In those days, we wore old wool uniforms with buttoned-down jerseys. The teams were sponsored by businesses whose names were displayed on the front of each jersey. The White Sox were sponsored by Data Machines Inc. and the letters 'DMI' were sewn vertically on the front of our jerseys. Like kids of all ages, the 'DMI' initials were translated into something more amusing and taunting, in this case 'Dumb Monkeys Incorporated'. All year long we had to put up with the taunts and jokes, but in the end we got even. The DMI White Sox would win the league championship two seasons in a row. My first manager on the White Sox was George Fransicshini, whose son played for the team. We had so much fun during those two seasons because our manager was so much fun. I recently had the pleasure of talking to him for the first time since 1965. He is 80 years old now but he still remembers that team and his players. One thing you always remember is your first little league manager and Mr. Francishini was so much fun he will never be forgotten...

Chapter 15: 'Time Jockey' – *The Early Gabrielenos* – By Joe Castillo (4/18/2008)

In this issue.... The beginnings of the Gabrielenos in the San Gabriel Valley; 'Lucky' Baldwin starting up racing on Rancho Santa Anita; interesting history in Vancouver; Monrovia Bee's; Pliny Temple settling down; and the Time Jockeys' World Series prediction.... ***Gabrieleno Beginnings*** .... The story of the Gabrielino Indians is one that has long been only half told. They were the first major inhabitants of Southern California and lived a proud, active and happy life. However, that all ended when the Spanish came into the area and sought to build a chain of missions throughout California in order to promote their way of life. Their history dates back nearly 7,000 years ago, over 5,000 years BC. Thought to be a branch of the Shoshone, the Gabrielenos came from the Great Basin of Southern Oregon and Nevada. The fertile lands of Southern California first attracted them to this area, but they were a coastal people with their early villages established along the coast. The name Gabrieleno was given them by the Spanish which usually named the Indians around a Mission after the name of the mission itself. The Gabrielenos lived by gathering roots, seeds, and fruits; fishing and harvesting shellfish; and hunting some deer and antelope. Their lands covered 4,000 square miles with boundaries of the San Bernardino and San Gabriel Mountains. From the shores of Long Beach all lands and sea for 50 miles in all directions were inhabited by the Gabrielenos. Even when the Spanish first explored California in the early 1600's, the Gabrielenos were well-established in the area and were at the peak of their existence....***Racetrack History ....*** As previously mentioned, E. J. 'Lucky' Baldwin first established 'formal' horse racing in Southern California. Racing of horses had always taken place since the days of the Spanish but Baldwin was the person who really wanted to make it into a business. Baldwin was known as a smart businessman with an eye at turning ventures into successes. He didn't always make money on his investments, but he rarely lost a significant amount of his investment on a deal gone sour. His biggest gain was the selling of his investment in the Ophir Mine for $5 million, which was a gain of over 500% of his original investment. Using the money wisely, he purchased Rancho Santa Anita for $200,000 from owner Harris Newmark. The story goes that Newmark knew Baldwin wanted to purchase Rancho Santa Anita, and knew that Baldwin made a sizeable gain with his sale of Ophir Mine stock. Baldwin had planned to make an offer to Newmark for $160,000, which was almost a 100% gain from the purchase price paid by Newmark. When Baldwin showed up to make his offer, Newmark refused and said the price was $180,000. Baldwin was stunned and went to talk with his lawyer, who recommended he pay the price if he really wanted Rancho Santa Anita. Baldwin again went to arrange a deal with Newmark, but this time the price was $200,000. After a short discussion with choice words, Baldwin knew if he left without ownership of Rancho Santa Anita, the sale price would continue to escalate. Baldwin agreed to the price and opened a black tin box which he carried under his arm. He then counted out $200,000 and paid cash for Rancho Santa Anita. According to Newmark, Baldwin kept over $1 Million dollars in that black tin box and placed it under his carriage seat when traveling in his buggy. Amazingly, no record was ever made of him being robbed…. ***Historical Vancouver ….*** On a recent trip to Vancouver, Canada, I had the pleasure of visiting the Christ Church Cathedral. The Cathedral was first built in 1888 and has since been fully restored with a cedar roof and fir flooring. I found the church interesting in a couple of ways. First, throughout the church were commemorations to Vancouver's and British Columbia's soldiers who gave their lives from conflicts before World War I or the First Great War, as it is called in Canada. Secondly, the stained glass windows are perhaps the finest I have ever seen. There are 30 windows throughout the cathedral with some covering more than one pane. One window is a scene of the Crucifixion and covers five panes. It was originally commissioned in 1911 at a cost of $1,100. Once completed, the windows were shipped from England, piece by piece, in barrels of molasses…. ***Beal's Bee's …..***In 1866, M.D. Beal became the first man to settle his family in the area which would become Monrovia. Mr. Beal was a rancher who raised bees. His ranch was in Cloverleaf Canyon. The Beal children went to

school in Savannah, which was a settlement near El Monte, California.... ***Temple Times ....*** Pliny Fisk Temple was born on Feb. 12, 1841 and was the youngest brother to John Temple. In 1841, Pliny boarded the American vessel 'Tasso', captained by Sam J. Hastings. They arrived in California with cargo of $15,000 but a duty to pay of $16,000, which showed in those days a minimal percent of profit from shipping. Also in 1841, the Workman-Rowland party arrived in Los Angeles from Santa Fe, New Mexico, which was part of Mexico at that time. The Workman-Rowland Party was the first immigrant party to travel the trade route to Southern California. Workman and Rowland applied for a land grant from the Spanish government and sought some of the former San Gabriel Mission lands. The La Puente Land Grant of 48,000 acres in the San Gabriel Valley was awarded to William Workman and John Rowland. Some time later, Pliny Temple met William Workman, and was introduced to his daughter, and eventually they married. Pliny Temple became William Workman's son-in-law and the Temple name became tied to one of the largest land owners in the San Gabriel Valley....
Baseball Prediction... With apologies to the Dodgers, I like Arizona and the Angels in the World Series, with Philadelphia and Toronto as my dark horse specials. Feel free to laugh but remember my Super Bowl prediction.... ***Final Quotes...*** '...*the garden city of the valley*'... an early reference to the City of El Monte.

63

Chapter 16:   'Time Jockey' – *Rancho Wolfskill* – By Joe Castillo (04/25/08)

In this issue- William Wolfskill buys Rancho Santa Anita; the Gabrieleno name; facts about Richard Nixon; Ranchos in Rosemead; and farewell to Jess Alvarado. ***William Wolfskill ....*** In 1865, Wolfskill and Leonard Rose each purchased subdivided parts of Rancho Santa Anita, with Wolfskill acquiring over 11,000 acres of the prime acreage for $20,000. Wolfskill was from Kentucky and arrived in Mexico California in 1831. He was a horticulturist, who developed the first commercial grape in California, and in 1856 was deemed to have the best vineyard in the state. In 1862, Wolfskill owned two-thirds of all orange trees in California. With his purchase of Rancho Santa Anita, Wolfskill and his expertise were seen as a perfect match to make the rancho prosperous again. But one year later, Wolfskill took ill and his life was cut short. In that short year, he only had time to do one thing, plant Eucalyptus trees, which still exist today on Santa Anita property. Wolfskill's son, Louis, took over ownership of Rancho Santa Anita and soon the increase of American businesses turned the rancho into valuable property. The price of land continued to escalate throughout Southern California, and Louis began to sell off parcels of Rancho Santa Anita in order to increase his profits. Alfred Chapman purchased 1,700 acres on the west boundary for $19,800, nearly the same price his father paid Hugo Reid for over 11,000 acres nearly 3 years before. Chapman's property would later be called Chapman Woods, as it is still called today. Louis Wolfskill offered the majority of his property, especially around the Reid homestead and lake, for sale. In 1870, Rancho Santa Anita was offered for sale at $9.00 an acre, by 1872 it had increased to $10.50 an acre. Finally, a Los Angeles merchant, Harris Newmark, purchased the entire rancho for less than $10 per acre. Newmark had learned of a proposal to build a railroad adjacent to Rancho Santa Anita and sensed an increase in value of his recent investment. With no intention of developing the rancho, Newmark held on to the property, hoping eventually to turn a hefty profit with a big sale. Enter E.J. 'Lucky' Baldwin, who after some shrewd negotiating by Newmark, purchased Rancho Santa Anita for $25 an acre, a 150% increase in what Newmark paid just a few years earlier. ***Naming the Gabrielenos*** .... Mission San Gabriel Archangel was named by the Spanish missionaries after the Archangel Gabriel, the angel who could foretell the future. The Gabrieleno Indians, who lived in the San Gabriel Valley and built the mission, were named after the mission. This was a common practice by the Spanish, who named the Gabrieleno neighboring tribes to the South after Mission San Juan Capistrano (Juaneno) and Mission San Luis Rey (Luiseno). Other neighboring tribes used their native names as no missions were built within their boundaries. To the east were the Mojaves, and to the North, the Chumash, the most advanced people in Southern California. The Chumash, who may have been in California up to 4,000 years prior to the arrival of the Gabrielenos, were master canoe builders and taught their trade to the Gabrielenos. This led to the exploration and settlement of the Channel Islands by the Gabrielenos, as well as developing their fishing expertise. The Gabrielenos began to grow and their economy expanded as a result of increased trade with other Southern California tribes, and in time the Gabrielenos became the 2nd wealthiest people, after the Chumash, in all California. ***Nixon Notes*** ... Here's some interesting facts on Richard Nixon. He was born in his family home in Yorba Linda, on his parents' bed.... He also was responsible for starting NASA, and was in office for all of the historic moon walks. ***Rose Village*** ... Monterey Pass Road, previously known as Coyote Pass, was the location of a large Gabrieleno village. The location was called 'Place of the Roses', based on the Indian word 'Otsur' for the large number of rose blooms in the near vicinity. ***Rosemead Ranchos***... During the rancho days, the present city of Rosemead was home to four ranchos: San Antonio, La Merced, Potrero Grande and Potrero Chico. ***Cattle Trail*** .... Mission Drive in San Gabriel and Rosemead follows the 1850 cattle trail route from the San Gabriel Mission to El Monte, which at that time was the only non-Spanish speaking settlement between Los Angeles and San Bernardino. ***Noteworthy ....*** Jess Alvarado, a longtime resident of San Gabriel, passed away recently at the age of 83. Jess was born in Los Angeles in 1924 and shortly thereafter moved to San Gabriel, where he married and raised his family. He graduated from Lincoln Grammar School and was attending Mark Keppel High School when the doors first opened in 1940. During World War II, he enlisted in the Army and was stationed at various bases, traveling throughout the U.S., Europe and Asia. Always a hard worker with an endless work ethic, Jess worked at numerous jobs to make ends meet including various positions at the San Gabriel Country Club and San Gabriel Nursery. He used his guitar playing talents to serenade guests, including Clark Gable and Dan Blocker, at the historic El Poche and Panchito's Restaurants on Mission Drive in San Gabriel. Jess worked for 37 years at The Standard Felt Company, while also doubling his hours working at the Pep Boys Auto Parts Store in Alhambra. Eventually, he finished his working career with the City of Alhambra, working well into his 70's. However, he may have missed his true calling because his storytelling was incomparable. Using a combination of English words and Spanish phrases, he turned the blandest of stories into a colorful, humorous and entertaining tale. Jess produced his own language and always added facial expressions and hand gestures to paint the perfect picture. But of all the stories I heard him tell, I never heard him tell a sad or serious one. He was always making people laugh with his stories, always wanting them to have a good time. Jess will be truly missed by Lillian, his wife of 62 years, his family and his many friends. None of them will ever forget his many stories which brought smiles to their faces, laughter to their voices and joy to their hearts. Rest in Peace, Nino Jess.

'Doc' Strub .... The history of Santa Anita Racetrack has to include Dr. Charles 'Doc' Strub. Always interested in sports, Strub had played baseball for the University of California at Berkeley. He was good enough to be named captain during his senior season and goon to play pro baseball.... But he had earned a Doctorate of Dental Surgery from UC Berkeley and left baseball to start his own dentist business. However, Strub was not only a dentist but a knowledgeable businessman who had a knack for success. Dr. Strub opened up numerous dentist offices and his popularity soon made Strub a very rich man.... Using his earnings, he organized a group of investors to purchase the San Francisco Seal Minor League Baseball Club. In 1917, he became the President of the organization and held the position of 18 years.... In those days, each minor league organization signed its own players to a contract. If a major league team wanted a player, they needed to purchase the contract from the minor league organization. A minor league organization's profit was not based on its winning record and ticket sales; it was based on the number of player contracts it sold to the major leagues. This is where 'Doc' Strub excelled.... Using his baseball experience, Strub wisely scouted, selected and signed young baseball players to contracts with the Seals. Prior to Strub's involvement in baseball, players were sold for $5,000 - $10,000 each. After Strub became involved, player contracts were sold for as much as $125,000 each. This included San Francisco Seal players such as Paul Waner, Lefty Gomez, and Joe and Dom DiMaggio. During his Presidency, 'Doc' Strub brought in over $1,000,000 from player contract sales for the San Francisco Seals. He would later use his money wisely and invest it in another sports related enterprise, the Los Angeles Turf Club.... ***Mesmerizing Baldwin ....*** Prior to purchasing Rancho Santa Anita, E.J. 'Lucky' Baldwin arrived in Southern California intending to invest in gold mines. Fresh off his huge investment gain in the Ophir Mine, Baldwin had money to invest. He had heard that gold was found in the San Bernardino Mountains and property was available near Big Bear Lake.... Arriving

67

in Los Angeles, Baldwin got a miserable night of sleep due to the loud noises outside his hotel window. But he was determined to check out property in Bear Valley. Traveling east through the San Gabriel Valley, he took the road which went through Rancho Santa Anita…. He found the ranch very much to his liking, and unlike Los Angeles, the ranch was quiet. Baldwin, who always had an eye for a good investment, noticed the quality of soil and   convinced he had found paradise, became determined to own Rancho Santa Anita…..
Portola's View… In 1769, Gaspar de Portola led an expedition   to the north from Baja California. With him was Father Junipero Serra, the Franciscan order priest who would go on and establish the California Missions…. Portola had been named governor of Alta and Baja California by King Carlos III in 1768. He was the first ruler of the province of Alta California, more as a military commander than as a civil governor, until July 9, 1770. King Carlos had sent Portola to the Baja to reclaim the missions from the Jesuits and return them to the Franciscan priests. Serra was the President of the Franciscan Missions from 1769 – 1784. …***Law and Order …..*** In 1869, Los Angeles established its first police department. The first police chief, or City Marshall as he was called, was William C. Warren, who was killed in a gun battle with one of his own deputies…. Warrens' future grandson, Eugene Biscailuz, would become sheriff of Los Angeles County. The collection of items he acquired during his time as sheriff was bequeathed to the Native Sons of the Golden West Ramona Parlor #109, where it is now displayed in the Biscailuz Room within the museum itself….***Campaigning in Monrovia…*** Before his election to Congress in 1946, and afterward, former President Richard Milhous Nixon was a frequent visitor to the city of Monrovia. His famous debate with Representative Jerry Voorhis took place at the Monrovia High School auditorium. Afterwards, Mr. and Mrs. Nixon entertained guests   at an afternoon reception at the Women's Clubhouse on Canyon Blvd…. ***Comments*** …. Please send all comments, suggestions or historical stories to joeacastillo@aol.com…. ***Noteworthy ….*** This month marks the 40th anniversary of a rare feat in Little League Baseball. In 1968, at Wells Park in San Gabriel, Steve Juarez, a crafty right-handed pitcher for

the Gemco Gems of the San Gabriel Eastern Little League, pitched a perfect game…. Pitching against the Prudential Savers, Juarez struck out 16 of the 18 batters he faced. Only two Saver batters did not strike out and both hit weak grounders back to Juarez for easy outs…. The historical feat was only the beginning for Juarez in his baseball career. Juarez would go on and pitch for the San Gabriel High School Matadors and the 1979 Cal State Los Angeles Diablo Baseball team, which went on to play in the N.C.A.A. Division I College World Series. Juarez pitched in the independent minor leagues before turning his attention to the game of golf …. Coincidently, Juarez' uncle was former Los Angeles Dodgers pitcher Hank Aguirre. I'm sure that Uncle Hank taught Steve some of the finer points of pitching because Steve always threw a pitch that somehow avoided your bat and swing…..

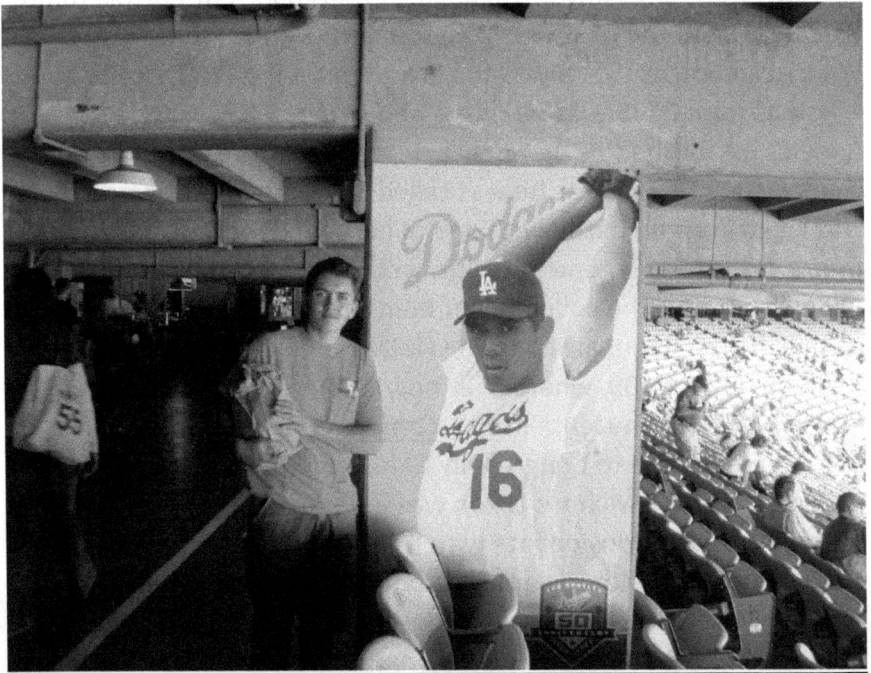

Chapter 18:   'Time Jockey' – *Historical Ramona* – By Joe Castillo (05-25-08)

Ramona …. The Ramona Outdoor Play celebrated its Jubilee 85th season this year. It is the longest running outdoor drama first opening on April 13, 1923, in the Hemet hillsides. Ramona is based on the novel *'Ramona'* by Helen Hunt Jackson, who wrote the book in 1884. Jackson had become the foremost writer of Native American rights and had spent a considerable amount of time researching the treatment of Indians by the United States Government. She called for changes in the government's Indian policies and documented their past crimes in her 1881 book, *'A Century of Dishonor'*…. But Jackson wanted everyday people to understand the plight of the Native Americans and wrote Ramona to enlighten them on the current situation. Even though most people view the story as a romance between two Indians, Ramona and Alessandro, it actually sends a social message showing the injustice, mistreatment and land theft against Indians by the American government and settlers…. The novel and play produced a sympathetic 'Ramona' effect on those who read the book and viewed the play. Soon the name 'Ramona' was incorporated throughout Southern California in schools, streets and public buildings. In San Gabriel, Ramona Avenue runs from the San Gabriel Mission south to Valley Blvd and 15 other streets throughout the San Gabriel Valley are named 'Ramona'. There are only two streets in the San Gabriel Valley named after Alessandro, with one being in Temple City. As a matter of fact, Cloverly Ave. also in Temple City used to be named Ramona Avenue, putting the name of the two main characters in the original city design …. ***Prosperity* ….** Under the guidance of 'Lucky' Baldwin, who had become a very good businessman, Rancho Santa Anita took a turn toward being a very lucrative enterprise. With his sizeable amount of assets, Baldwin used his businessman knowledge to become the first President of the Pacific Stock Exchange. In addition, he saved the Bank of California from collapse after President William Ralston committed suicide…. But Rancho Santa Anita was where his real business interests were. Baldwin employed over 300 persons at the rancho, mostly Chinese, Mexicans and Americans, at a rate of $1 per day. Field hands were paid $25 per month including boarding and skilled laborers were paid $35 per month including boarding.... During its peak, the rancho produced 384,000 gallons of wine per year, 55,000 gallons of brandy, 175,000 sacks of grain, 44,000 crates of oranges and lemons and the first walnut crops in Southern California. The livestock on the rancho included 33,000 sheep, 3,000 cattle, 50 mules and 500 horses, 70 of which were race horses.... But Baldwin owned more property than the central location of the rancho. His holdings were included the present areas and cities of San Marino, Arcadia, Monrovia, Lamada Park, Chapman Woods, Sierra Madre, Azusa, Baldwin Park, El Monte and parts of Baldwin Hills, Angeles Mesa, Leimart Park, and View Park.... However, Baldwin's passion was horse racing and his stable was considered one of the best in the world. The Maltese Cross was used as the symbol of Baldwin's racing stable and was placed on the silks of the jockeys riding his horses. The cornerstone of Baldwin's stable is the great horse Volante. In the 1880's, Volante won 35 of 84 races, with 35 finishes of 2nd or 3rd place. Baldwin initiated the American Derby and in 1885 Volante won the inaugural event. Baldwin's passion with horses and horse racing, led him to his ultimate goal, building his own racetrack. His goal was achieved when construction was completed and the racetrack was opened in December 1907. The site was south of the present location of Santa Anita Racetrack, and a short ride from Baldwin's residence. On March 1, 1909, Baldwin died, leaving behind his horses, racetrack and vast real estate holdings to his estate and family.... ***The Moving Wall ....*** I hope you had a chance to visit the 'Moving Wall' while it was at Temple City Park May 15 -18. The Moving Wall is a half-size replica of the Vietnam Veterans Memorial in Washington, D.C. and travels throughout the country to be displayed for all to see, hence the name 'moving'. But I think that it's named after the affect the wall has on you.... To see the names of over 58,000 American soldiers killed in Vietnam between 1959 and 1975 is truly overwhelming and moving. I remember when I saw the Memorial in Washington D.C. in 1986. It had an affect on me that I will never forget. Fellow veterans and friends of those listed on the memorial were crying, talking or sharing a drink with the memories of those on the wall. There was a respectful silence in the near proximity, with no idle chatter or talk or cell phones to break up the solitude. It was like an outdoor church…. The 58,000 young men and women were the most killed in any American conflict. In 1968 alone, over 16,000 Americans were killed…. I talked to Ignacio Zarate of El Monte, a Vietnam Veteran, who was a volunteer at the memorial. Zarate served in the U.S. Army, 3rd Airborne Division during 1967-1968. He was involved in combat, and proudly displayed his combat badge for us. He remembered seeing the Vietnamese people struggling to survive in poverty, similar to what he saw growing up in the states. Zarate shipped out to Vietnam from Travis Air Force Base in Sacramento. In the days just before being shipped out, the Army provided the best, all-you-can-eat meals to the outbound soldiers. These final meals while in the states would become known as the 'Last Supper'…. Today, Zarate is a volunteer at the Veterans Hospital in Los Angeles, helping veterans to overcome physical injuries and disabilities. It is on Memorial Day we remember those who gave their lives for our country but we should also be grateful to men like Ignacio Zarate who served and continue to serve their country by helping fellow comrades and taking the time to share his story for all of us to understand …. ***Original…..*** Los Angeles County was originally created with 6 townships: Los Angeles, San Gabriel, San Jose, San Bernardino, Santa Ana and San Juan. ***Street Guide…*** Peck Ave. in El Monte is named after George S. Peck, who came from Vermont and settled in San Francisco. He mined for a time and then started handling hay for $200 per ton. He opened the first industrial complex in San Francisco and then the first public school in Sacramento…. He moved to Southern California in 1869 and bought 500 acres near El Monte. Peck was named Los Angeles County Superintendent of Schools in 1874 and established the foundation for what would become one of the largest educational systems in the United States….***This Day in History ….*** On June 2, 1935, baseball great Babe Ruth retired after 22 major league seasons. Ruth retired holding nearly every important major league batting record, including career home runs with 714....

Chapter 19: 'Time Jockey' – *Sheriff Gene* – By Joe Castillo (06-21-08)

In this issue….. A look at one of Los Angeles County's best sheriffs; the Gabrieleno presence in Altadena; Los Angeles Turf Club's prosperous investment; 'Lucky' Baldwin's estate home; the UCLA mascot; Ryan Tucker's blazing trail through major league baseball and Native Sons of the Golden West award winners….. *Golden Sheriff ….* This year marks the 50th year since Los Angeles County Sheriff Eugene W. Biscailuz retired after serving as Sheriff for 26 years and a member of the L.A. County Sheriff's Department for 50 years. When Biscailuz became a deputy in 1907, only 27 deputies were employed in the department. When he retired 50 years later, the department had grown to 3,000 and was serving over 2 million people in the unincorporated areas of Los Angeles County…. During his tenure as Sheriff, one of Biscailuz's great accomplishments was solving a robbery in Temple City. On February 17, 1955, a large restaurant in Temple City was robbed of its floor size safe and a large amount of currency. By noon of the next day, sheriff deputies had the suspects in custody and the safe and money were safely returned to the restaurant owner….. *Mapping Alta California….* Alta California included present day California, Arizona, Utah and Nevada and parts of Wyoming, Colorado and New Mexico. The Russians were coming in from the North, with fur trapping and whaling expeditions and the Spanish wanted to secure its holdings by establishing a string of Missions in Alta California. During Portola's first expedition in 1769, his men climbed the San Rafael Hills of Pasadena in order to try and find their bearings in the new land. From their vantage point, they saw a large village just west of the Arroyo among the oak tree groves. These were the Hahamonga people, a branch of the Gabrielenos. The tribe also inhabited areas of Milliard and Eaton Canyons. The Hahamonga people were the first indigenous people of the Altadena-Pasadena area and Chief Hahamongvic was their leader…. Portola's second trip in 1770, returned him to the same area and this time he named the Altadena area *Sabanilla de San Pasqual* (Altar Cloth of Holy Easter). Portola named and christened Hahamongvic, *Pasqual El Capitan,* and called his people *Pasqual...* Years later, the original land grant of the Altadena and Pasadena area listed the area as Rancho San Pasqual....***Magic Turf....*** Dr. Charles 'Doc' Strub, along with Hal Roach, spearheaded an investment group to form the Los Angeles Turf Club and bring formalized horse racing to Southern California. Strub became the General Manager and Vice President, while Roach was named President. The group raised enough money to purchase 200 acres of 'Lucky' Baldwin's former property and then drew additional investors to purchase another 400 acres adjacent to their initial purchase...... Using his great business sense, Strub sold shares of LA Turf Club for $5,000 each. Within a year, the popularity of the sport and its location in Southern California increased the value of each share to $75,000 each. After the first year, shareholders received another pleasant surprise, a dividend payment of $75,000.... The increased value of his initial investment group allowed Strub to offer purses never before seen in the horse racing industry. Santa Anita became the first racetrack to offer a $100,000 purse in a handicap, derby, 4-year old exclusive race and grass turf classic races. The premier race became the Santa Anita Handicap, offered as a $100,000 race in its initial running. Azucar, with George Woolf in the saddle, won the handicap on Feb. 23, 1935. Following the 1935 season, the popularity of the handicap, the large purses and the growth of thoroughbred horse racing, led the Los Angles Turf Club directors to approve a shareholder dividend of 55%....***The Estate Grows...*** As 'Lucky' Baldwin's ranch grew in prosperity, he began to funnel more cash into Rancho Santa Anita as well as provide loans for local investments.... Baldwin decided to build his Queen Anne Cottage next to the lake on his ranch's property. The Queen Anne Cottage accommodated Baldwin's visitors who wanted to spend some time on the rancho. The cottage was built on grounds   surrounded with exotic plants, large lawns, shaded walks, a well-stocked deer park and numerous peafowl, which were descendants of three pairs of peafowls Baldwin brought with him from India.... Today, the Queen Anne Cottage still stands on the Arboretum grounds pretty much as Baldwin had designed it and its surrounding landscape.... ***UCLA***

Mascot ... The University of California, Los Angeles (UCLA) was originally the southern branch of The University of California, which was known as Cal and its mascot was the Bear. In the 1930's, UCLA decided to become its own school and adopted the mascot of Bruins, a small and fierce version of the Bear ... ***The Tucker Trail .....*** Temple City High School Baseball Coach Barry Bacon has hinted that Ryan Tucker's high school jersey will be retired now that Tucker has made his major league baseball debut. Tucker's jersey number 22 is currently worn by junior catcher Ruben Jara, who was coached by Tucker in 2003 while with the Temple City American Little League Major Mariners ....Since his debut on June 6th, Tucker has started two additional games, losing 7-3 to the Tampa Bay Rays and then winning 8-3 against the Seattle Mariners, a game in which he showcased his 96 MPH fastball. For the season, he has 2 wins and 1 loss, with a 4.50 ERA giving up 8 earned runs in 16 innings, while also getting 12 KO's....... Tucker has earned a starting spot in the 5-man Marlin rotation and his next start is projected to be against the team which handed him his only loss of the season, the Tampa Bay Rays.... ***Noteworthy ....*** The Native Sons of the Golden West Ramona Parlor #109 presented their annual awards at their anniversary barbeque. Frank Claro, longtime member and former president of the association, received the Grizzly Bear statue symbolic of the member of the year. Joey Castillo received a $100 Gift certificate for volunteer of the year, having given numerous hours in helping in and around the museum and with the organization's activities..... The Ramona Parlor and Museum is located in San Gabriel and is dedicated to preserving the history of California.... ***This Day in History....*** June 23, 1967, American runner Jim Ryun lowered the world record in the mile to 3:51.1 .....

Chapter 20: 'Time Jockey' - *Happy Birthday, Juan!* – By Joe Castillo (07-06-08)

Sanchez Adobe …. The City of Montebello and the Montebello Historical Association celebrated the 200th birthday of Juan Sanchez at the Juan Matias Sanchez Historic Site and Museum in Montebello on Saturday June 28th. The celebration included entertainment, cultural presentations, historical group displays, historical re-enactments and food…. The adobe was built in 1845 and is the oldest building in the Montebello area. Under the guidance of the Montebello Building Department and the direction of Ron Bustamonte, the adobe has been fully restored and upgraded… Inside the adobe was a collection of furniture pieces from the era as well as other pieces on loan from the Los Angeles County Museum of History.   A small kitchen area in the adobe was used to keep cooked food warm. The actual kitchen was located approximately 2 blocks away, where 3-4 sheep were cooked daily and then taken to the smaller kitchen or *azador*. The bedroom furniture included a standing closet, which was also a sign of people of wealth. When the closet was first acquired docents attempted numerous times to open it but were unable to do so. Days later it opened by itself without any assistance perhaps getting some sort of unnatural assistance…. The family history of Juan Sanchez is chronicled in detail and well displayed throughout the museum. Sanchez, who was married twice, built the adobe and lived in it with both his families until his death….Gabrieleno Spiritual leader Ernie Salas made a presentation on the Gabrieleno culture and blessed the event with a prayer and the releasing of two doves. While growing up, Salas lived with his father in the adobe and would walk to nearby Temple School each day. The Gabrielenos' display included authentic artifacts: turtle shells, diamondback rattlesnakes, rams' hoofs, a willow branch clapper, acorn grinding bowls and children's rattles made from gourds…. All in all it was a very interesting, entertaining and well-organized event with enough activities and displays to keep everyone busy as well as educate those in attendance about Juan Sanchez and the history of the adobe … *Rancho Hey Days ….* Under 'Lucky' Baldwin's ownership, Rancho

Santa Anita reached its peak operating status. The Rancho had an abundance of crops, trees, livestock and grapes. Over 500 acres were orange groves; over 1 million trees were in the nursery with 3,000 English walnut trees.... Baldwin built a winery and produced over 384,000 gallons of wine and 55,000 gallons of brandy. The winery still stands at Santa Anita, overlooking the west end of the racetrack.... Grain and alfalfa were grown to feed the large number of livestock supported by the rancho which included 33,000 sheep, 3,000 cattle, 500 horses and large dairy herds. But over the next 20 years, nature took its toll on the success of the Baldwin's ranch. Rain, drought and insect infestation all reduced the capacity to produce crops and raise livestock. Baldwin became land rich and money poor.... But the land boom of the 1880's saved Baldwin and Rancho Santa Anita. Baldwin had an idea that large land sales would eventually take place in the valley so Baldwin contracted with the Santa Fe Railroad to stop at the Santa Anita Depot on his ranch. Baldwin had two motives in mind for signing the contract: to create a power play with the railroads and for passengers to see future home sites which Baldwin planned to sell from his Rancho Santa Anita property. With the introduction of the Santa Fe Railroad, the growth and expansion of towns, homes and people started to take place throughout the San Gabriel Valley..... ***Sports Shorts ....*** On July 21, 1969, Apollo 11, the first mission to place a man on the moon, blasted off from the moon for its return trip back to Earth. Here are some of the sports stories included in an old Alhambra Post Advocate newspaper on that date..... The San Francisco Giants beat the Dodgers 7-3 to move into a tie with the Dodgers for 2nd place in the Western Division, one game back of the Atlanta Braves. While the Giants lineup included future Hall Of Famers Willie Mays and Willie McCovey, the Dodgers were a notch below in the quality of their lineup. Maury Wills batted leadoff and Manny Mota batted second but the other players were pretty much average ballplayers. Incidentally, Mota was the starting centerfielder.... The Los Angeles Rams opened their first full-scale practice of the season, and all players except one reported to camp on time... District 18 Little League playoffs were in full swing. South Pasadena National,

Temple City National, El Monte National and San Gabriel National all won to advance to the district semi-finals. The entire lineups and box scores for each quarterfinal game were printed in the paper. In those days, the Little League All-Star Tournament was a single elimination event, which meant one loss would send you home..... The great Sandy Koufax had become a newspaper writer and wrote an article previewing the upcoming All-Star game in Washington D.C., home of the Senators. Koufax wrote the following comments on future Hall-of-Famer Hank Aaron, *'there's no one way to pitch to Hank. As Dizzy Dean once said, 'Give it your best and pray"*.....

Market Memories .... Here are some of advertised sales which were taking place at Hughes Market in Alhambra on July 16, 1969..... 'Choicest of the U.S.D.A. Choice '... Cube Steaks $1.29/ lb., New York Steaks $2.49/ lb., T-bone steak $1.49/lb. and Porterhouse Steaks $1.59 /lb.... Other items.... Central American Bananas... 9 cents/lb.... G&H Granulated Sugar, 5 lbs, 57 cents.... Tide XK Detergent Giant Size 69 cents/lb..... Now those were sales !!!!!...... ***Movie Madness....*** Movie theaters have changed considerably since the early days of the 60's. Edwards Theater actually got its start right here in the San Gabriel Valley. The first Edwards Movie House was at the San Gabriel Mission Playhouse and shortly thereafter Edwards expanded throughout the valley.... In 1969, Edwards had the following locations: San Gabriel Drive-In on Valley Blvd; Edwards Drive-In at Peck Rd. and Live Oak in Arcadia; Foothill Drive-In on Foothill Blvd in Azusa; Edwards Alhambra Cinema, Main St at Atlantic; Edwards El Rey, Main St. at 4th in Alhambra; Edwards Capri, Main St. and 2nd in Alhambra; Edwards Monterey, on Garfield in Monterey Park; Edwards Temple at Las Tunas and Rosemead in Temple City; and Edwards Century on Las Tunas in San Gabriel. .... There were nine Edwards' theaters with 5 locations on the Main St/Las Tunas roadway.... In July 1969, the major movies showing were Walt Disney's The Love Bug, Swiss Family Robinson, Winnie the Pooh, and Peter Pan ..... ***Comments ....*** Please send your comments to joeacastillo@aol.com. All comments and feedback are welcome... ***This Date in History ...*** On July 11, 1964, in the United

States, the first 7-11 convenience store opened. Its name is the result of its extended hours 7AM – 11 PM....

Chapter 21:   'Time Jockey' – *A Dream Visit to Dodger Stadium* – By Joe Castillo (7/12/08)

Dreams …. Temple City's Ryan Tucker made his Dodger Stadium debut pitching for the Florida Marlins last Thursday. I've known Ryan since he was 10 years old and from the first time I met him he wanted to play professional baseball. Early last month, he was called up to the major leagues and now he was coming to play in the stadium where he probably saw his first major league game and dreamed of playing on the same field one day. This was his day, a day to be seen by his family and many friends. But even though Ryan was the one everyone was coming to see, it was also a special day for me. I've managed and coached Little League Baseball for most of 25 years. Almost every player I coached dreamed of playing professional baseball. But of all the kids I coached none of them until Ryan had made the Major Leagues. Some were drafted and signed by major league clubs, some played college ball, but none made the big show. So to see Ryan pitch at Dodger Stadium was something I had longed to see, something every coach wishes for his players. It was made more special as I was allowed to cover his Dodger Stadium debut as a journalist. So I get to write about Ryan and about my special day at Dodger Stadium. Here is my story just as it took place ….***Thursday July 10, 3:36 PM ….*** I pick-up my fellow San Gabriel Valley Weekly journalist Jaimi Harrison and carpool to the game. Jaimi has covered the Dodgers for the newspaper before and tonight she will show me the ropes. She has already warned me that I won't be home until midnight and to be ready to do a lot of walking…. ***4:07 PM …***We arrive at Dodger Stadium and park in the top deck parking with all the other press cars and I'm told some players also park here. We check-in and pickup our press passes. I notice a plaque on the stadium wall 'Dedication of Dodger Stadium April 14, 1962', over 46 years ago …. ***4:23 PM…*** We ride the elevator down to the Club Level. According to the elevator operator, there are 9 levels or floors at the Stadium. We go down to the Vin Scully Press Room on the 5th floor where we pick a spot on writer's row. The front row is reserved for the big newspapers, like the Los Angeles Times, and any unmarked spot is open to anyone else. The Press Room is named after Dodger broadcaster Vin Scully, who has been their voice since 1949, over 58 years, even longer than Dodger Stadium has been around.... ***4:28 PM*** .... We go down to the field where the Dodgers are taking batting and fielding practice. Bullpen coach Jim Slaton is pitching to the pitchers. Chad Billingsley is in the cage, followed by Jason Schmidt, Derek Lowe, Hiroki Kuroda. Schmidt looks like a seasoned veteran, while Billingsley looks right out of high school. Lowe is a lot taller than he appears on television and actually looks more like a golfer. Around the batting cage are two Hall Of Fame managers, Tommy Lasorda and Joe Torre, along with Dodger great Don Newcombe. I want to go up and interview them but they look like they're actually coaching the batters.... ***4:31 PM***.... I walk over to the Dodger Dugout. People are milling around and only a couple of people are sitting on the bench. I decide to sit there to check out the view from the bench. I sit down and gaze out at the field. My eye level is at the same level as the field itself. It's a subterranean view and even though I don't like it, maybe it takes a time to get used to it .... ***4:34 PM*** ... As I sit on the bench, in comes Dodger Manager Joe Torre, who says 'Alright guys, where do you want me to sit?' He sits three feet to my left to do his pregame interview with the press. About 15 reporters gather around to ask Torre questions and listen to his responses. His hat is tipped back on his forehead; he holds a cup in his right hand. I notice no championship rings and definitely no glitzy jewelry. Torre answers questions patiently, smoothly and professionally; his responses are insightful and genuine. On Jonathan Broxton being a closer sometime in his career, '... it's not a reach. He's got that kind of stuff'. But he cautions that even Mariano Rivera struggled when moved from the setup man to closer, 'there is no safety net when pitching in that role.' Torre tells us that many of his decisions are based on what he see's and feels and not just statistics. He tells the story of using Wade Boggs as a pinch hitter in a close game. Torre never looked at any numbers and only saw the former batting champion as being the most likely player to provide a clutch hit. But Boggs struck out on 3 pitches and as Torre says, 'I'll take my chances'. He notes as an afterthought that Boggs probably was asked to pinch hit very little during his career. Torre answered every question coolly and calmly, the respect between him and the press is clearly evident. The interview winds down after 15 minutes .... *4:53 PM*... I meet and shake hands with Tommy Lasorda, who attends as many Dodger games as he can. We ask what he'll do during the upcoming All-Star break. He replies the he's going to the game and that all the Hall Of Famers will be honored in a special ceremony... *4:56 PM*... We go visit the Marlin's clubhouse. We pass Dodger announcer Charley Steiner along the way and say 'Hi!' I say to myself, 'he doesn't look like his voice' ... *5:17 PM*... The Marlins arrive on the field to take batting and fielding practice. We interview Batting Coach Jim Presley about the pitchers taking batting practice. He says that on the road, only the starting pitchers take BP and they take it after everyone else. At home, both the starters and relievers take batting practice. I notice pitcher Scott Olsen walking by us. He sure looks young and I find out later he's only 24 years old .... *5:30 PM*.... We visit the nearly deserted Dodger Clubhouse. The player's lockers are approximately 4-feet wide and 8-feet tall and are all lined up along the walls. A couple of sofas sit in the middle of the room with 3 wide-screen TV's hanging from the ceiling. The showers are located at the far end of the clubhouse and the offices are at the opposite end. A wooden bat rack with the teams in the National League West is mounted on the clubhouse wall. The Dodgers are at the top in first place. A small sign at the front of the entrance wall reads 'The Road to the World Series Begins Here'. ... *5:32 PM*... I meet Manny Mota in the clubhouse. Even though over 60 years old, he looks like a veteran player. I ask him about a 1969 box score which listed him as the starting centerfielder for the Dodgers. He says he never played center, only left field.... *5:34 PM*.... Jonathan Broxton walks by, he is much bigger than he appears on TV.... *5:40PM*... Back on the field, I find out from security personnel that the stadium and field operations take place on a tight schedule. At 5:10, one gate at Dodger Stadium is opened for anyone who wants to come in and see batting practice. At 5:40, all other parking and stadium gates are opened .... *5:41 PM*... We meet and shake hands with Fernando

Valenzuela. I ask him how his golf game is going and he says it stinks. .. ***6:36 PM*** … Kareem is sighted in the field level boxes…..
6:43 PM … I talk with security guard Richard who says that the most popular teams are the interleague and East coast teams who only come out once a season. Richard ought to know, he's been in the same Dodger security position for 26 years…. ***6:48 PM***… The field crew is spray painting the batters box, foul lines and the bases…
7:02 PM….. Bob Harrison of Green Street Restaurant is sighted in the field level. I visit him for a few minutes and then leave to go up to the press box. .. ***7:04 PM*** … A cute young lady shows me her ticket and asks me how to get to her seat. I say 'I'm not sure, I don't work here'. She says 'Oh, but you have a badge on.. .' …. ***7:14 PM***…I arrive at the Press Box. The cafeteria offers free drinks and a $7 buffet. I'm so thirsty I get two ice teas. My backpack, which I left up there almost 3 hours ago, is exactly where I left it…. ***7:16 PM***… Matt Kemp makes the first Dodger error of the evening. The official announcement is made in the Press Box. … ***7:23 PM….***. Mike Jacobs hits into a Dodger double play. I cheer but no one else in the press box does. I think you're supposed to be neutral… ***7:27 PM***… I get the 'Hi' nod from Jim Hill Channel 2 Sportscaster, sitting behind me on press row… ***7:28 PM***… I count 40-45 reporters in the press box. There are only six who don't have a laptop, including myself and Jim Hill…. ***7:32 PM***… Marlin John Baker hits a home run, a towering shot to right field. It's his first career hit and home run as announced in the press box… ***7:40 PM…*** I notice the press box is like a dot com business, everyone typing on his keyboard and working at his job. Emails and cell phone calls are used to communicate with their newspaper and others in the outside world…. ***7:44 PM*** …. I take a guess at the attendance. With 2/3 of the seats filled, my guess is 40,000 – 45,000 fans but I can't really see the upper levels… ***8:15 PM***…. First beach ball of the evening lands on the field…. ***8:50 PM*** … I visit the Press Box cafeteria. Classic black and white photos of the Dodgers are enlarged, framed and placed on the walls. Similar types of pictures are found throughout the stadium, but especially in the press, clubhouse and stadium club areas.   My favorite photo is a 1970 spring training photo of Dodger players having a bicycle race.

Walter Alston is in the middle of the group and Steve Garvey, Wes Parker, Maury Wills and Bill Russell can all be seen ... ***9:43 PM*** .... Tonight's attendance is announced, 40,417. My guess was right on the numbers .... ***10:01 PM*** ... As the game slows down, writers are trying to finish up their stories and meet their deadlines. It looks like most of them have their stories done and are only waiting for the final outcome... ***10:51 PM....***. Top of the 11th inning, Marlin Shortstop Hanley Ramirez hits a home run to deep left field to put the Marlins up 5-4. It is Ramirez' 5th hit of the game, a career best. ... ***11:02 PM***... Dodger Shortstop Angel Berroa grounds out to end the game, 3 hours and 51 minutes after it started. The Press Box starts to slowly empty... ***11:31 PM*** ... I ride the elevator to the top level. Nomar Garciaparra and Russell Martin, wearing baseball caps, are also on the same ride.... ***12:01 AM*** .... I arrive home. I remember that Jaimi had said I would be home at midnight .... ***Postgame comments ....*** It was sure a long day but I'll never forget it. I saw so much and everyone from the players and coaches to the stadium employees and former players were extremely nice and friendly. It really was a once in a lifetime experience. Next season when Ryan and the Marlins visit Dodger Stadium, I've got to make sure I'm there again ......

Chapter 22: 'Time Jockey' – *Home Sweet Home* – By Joe Castillo (08/08/2008)

In this issue ..... A behind the scene tour of the Workman/Temple Houses and the Homestead Museum; San Gabriel Golf Legend Patrick Carrigan; 'Lucky' Baldwin's city, political and entrepreneur ventures; and an update on my baseball prediction... ***Behind the Scenes ....*** On occasion, the Homestead Museum in the City of Industry, offers a Behind the Scenes Tour of the ranch homes of William Workman and his grandson Walter P. Temple. The Homestead also offers regular tours of the restored and furnished areas of the homes but the Behind the Scenes Tours will go to those areas which the public rarely sees.... In 1841, William Workman and John Rowland received a 49,000 acre grant from the Mexican government and then split the acreage to develop it in their own way. Workman established a farm and built his ranch house as the center of the site. He originally built a home with three adobe rooms and between 1841 and 1850 added five rooms and followed by another five rooms for a grand total of 13 rooms..... In 1860, bricks started to be forged and Workman added even more rooms and to create it's current 'H-shape' ... After viewing the outside of the house, the tour went into the basement, which in the early days of the ranch was used as the kitchen to actually cook the food. The entrance to the kitchen in the basement was directly to the outside and did not go through the house. After the house changed ownership, a military academy used the basement, including the kitchen area, for classrooms.... Upstairs in the house, was the preparation kitchen with walls made of brick. The ceiling was 20 feet high and cabinets went all the way to ceiling. Inside the kitchen was a 30-foot well which was used to bring fresh water into the house. In 1868, Workman added a second story which was used mainly for storage. When the home changed ownership, the attic was changed into four large bedrooms to house students from the military academy.... Some other interesting notes on the Workman House was that the house had four chimneys but only two fireplaces, a rose plant in the garden was planted in 1860 by

Workman's granddaughter Lucinda, and Workman had three wineries on the property, two for wine and one for brandy…. The newer house, *La Casa Nueva*, was built by Workman's grandson Walter P. Temple. Temple restored his grandfather's house and then built a newer modern home next door for his wife and family. The home was made of adobe and was dedicated to the memory of his wife Laura, who died one year after construction of the home started. The main front door entrance is painted with symbolic images of the era including both the American and Mexican Eagles, Spanish columns and intertwined grape vines… The basement was well designed and constructed with a large full-sized safe and vault. The safe may have been used at Temple Bank in Los Angeles, and much later brought to the house and installed in the basement. It has a six-foot high door with a combination locking mechanism. Twenty people can easily fit into the vault, which contained air holes just in case someone got stuck in there. The cabinets in the vault were made of cedar to protect against mold and mildew. The safe was made by Diebold Safe and Lock Company in Canton, Ohio. Today, Diebold makes ATM units which are installed at many of our major local Banks…. The house originally had two patios upstairs which were converted into hospital rooms with the change of ownership. The new house contained 22 rooms and had only one telephone. There was no telephone in Temple's office known as the 'tee-pee' as Temple did not like telephones and preferred the quiet and solitude. Temple lost the home during the depression when his large financial investments were lost with the failure of the banking industry. The Brown's bought the property and the houses, and then it was sold to hospital and military school interests. Finally, the City of Industry purchased the property and established the Homestead Museum. Regular tours are offered every weekend and Behind the Scene Tours are offered on a seasonal schedule. For more information, call the museum at (626) 968-8492. …***Mission Golfer*** …. Patrick Carrigan, 1970 graduate of San Gabriel Mission Grammar School and 1974 graduate of Bishop Amat High School, recently competed in the USGA U.S. Senior Open Championship at The Broadmoor Golf Club in Colorado Springs, Colorado. Carrigan shot an opening round of 80 followed by a Round 2 score of 79, for 19 over par. He recorded 1 birdie, 19 pars and 12 bogeys for the 36 holes. He finished tied for 123rd of 155 golfers but just missed qualifying for the final two rounds…. Always an avid golfer, Carrigan qualified for the U.S. Senior Open by scoring a 70 in the sectional qualifying round at the SCGA Golf Course in Murrieta, California. He has played in three U.S. Amateurs (1989, 1990, 1994) and four U.S. Mid-American Amateurs (1988, 1998, 2005, 2006) ……He listed his most memorable shot as an Eagle 3 on the 543 yard-par 5 18th hole at Pebble Beach Golf Links. The eagle shot vaulted Carrigan into the final round of match play in the 1997 California State Amateur…. Years ago, I beat Carrigan straight-up in a very competitive 18-hole round. Even though it was at the Famous Aloha Miniature Golf Course in San Gabriel, it still qualifies as a highlight in my golf career and I'm especially glad that Pat has rebounded from that upset to reach new successes in his great and outstanding golf career …

Baldwin Dream …. With the development of the railroad in Southern California, 'Lucky' Baldwin foresaw the development of home and tract sites. Baldwin had taken notice of the plans by Nathaniel Carter (founder of Sierra Madre) and William Monroe (founder of Monrovia) and began moving in the same direction. He too, envisioned profits to be gained from the sale of individual tract lots and not the sale of large acreages. … At the age of 78, Baldwin laid out the plans to design the City of Arcadia and initiated a vote to incorporate the city. The story goes that there were not enough residents in Arcadia at that time to approve the initiative. Needing more residents, Baldwin received from Henry E. Huntington a loan of a number of workers, who moved into some of Baldwin's property and then acted as residents. The vote for incorporation was taken and passed with Arcadia becoming a city and Baldwin becoming the first mayor. He also envisioned plans of building and operating his own racetrack and in 1907 built one on the site of present day Arcadia Park, where over 20,000 fans attend opening day on Christmas Day, 1907. Fourteen months later, Mayor Baldwin died at his Lakeside home at Rancho Santa Anita…. ***Noteworthy*** ….. This past April, I printed my prediction for the upcoming baseball season, so here's an update on how it's going so far. In the American League, I predicted the Angels would win with the Toronto Blue Jays as my darkhorse. In the National League, I predicted Arizona would win with Philadelphia as my darkhorse…. As of last week, the Angels were in 1st place by 13 games in the West Division and Toronto was in 4th place in the East only 7 ½ games back of the Wild Card. Arizona led the West Division by 1 ½ games and Philadelphia led the East by 2 ½ games…. ***This date in History. …..*** On August 15, 1939, MGM's *The Wizard of Oz* has its premier at Grauman's Chinese Theater in Hollywood, California….

Chapter 23: 'Time Jockey' – A Street Named Dana – By Joe Castillo (8-29-08)

A Lasting Tribute .... This isn't the type of column I was expecting to write, nor is it a column that I really wanted to write. But sometimes we have to do things that we would rather not have to. You see, I write a historical column. A column based on historical facts, persons, places and events in the San Gabriel Valley. I've written about the San Gabriel Mission, 'Lucky' Baldwin, Santa Anita Racetrack, H. E. Huntington and the Gabrielenos. I've written about various related stories like haunted historical places, armed service veterans, the Rose Parade and baseball in the San Gabriel Valley. But this column will not be about a historically related topic, or anything historical of that matter. It will be about a dedicated and devoted family man, a hard-working businessman and journalist, and a guy with a unique sense of humor, strong values and even stronger opinions. This column will be about Dana Baskin, the owner, publisher, editor and nearly everything else of this newspaper, who passed away last week at the youthful age of 55. Throughout my numerous columns, I have written about people who have left their mark on our local and national history. People like H.E. Huntington, who built, established and lived in his mansion at the present day Huntington Library; Elias Jackson 'Lucky' Baldwin who owned and lived in his ranch located on the site of the present day Los Angeles County Arboretum in Arcadia; William Workman and Walter P. Temple, who owned and lived in their rancho estates located at the present day site of the Homestead Museum in the City of Industry; and Richard Nixon, 37th President of the United States, whose birthplace and library is in Yorba Linda and who grew up in nearby Whittier. These historical people are embedded into our local history through the names of towns, streets, and schools which carry their names. It's hard to drive through the valley and not run across a name of someone who did something extraordinary, who owned or developed acres of land, or who led such a quality life that he earned people's admiration and respect. These influential and important people are memorialized throughout our cities, and rightfully so as they had an enormous impact on the development of this region. Dana Baskin, was not a war hero, did not own thousands of acres of prime San Gabriel Valley land, did not own a racetrack or racehorse for that matter, and was not a political figure who proposed a civil rights, education or immigration measure which would change the quality of life for thousands of underprivileged persons. He didn't appear to be a multi-millionaire, a large national business owner, a rich oil man, or a prosperous rancher with a large number of crops and livestock. Dana was an ordinary guy, a family man who also happened to own a newspaper. The San Gabriel Valley Weekly, and the Temple City Weekly before that, was Dana's commitment and life. For 10 plus years, Dana was publisher, editor, writer, salesman, distributor, heart and soul of this publication. It was his newspaper. He chose the design, edited the stories, formatted the articles, cropped the pictures, produced the drafts, obtained the printing and delivered the paper for us to read each week. He was a throwback to another newspaper era. He may have used a computer instead of a type setter, and a car instead of a horse and buggy, but make no mistake about it, he was as committed and dedicated to producing his local newspaper on his own as any other early American newspaper publisher. It was a hard job, requiring long hours and meeting deadlines, but getting his paper out on time every time was his primary goal and objective. The San Gabriel Valley Weekly is distributed to nine valley cities. It provides a variety of articles from recent and upcoming local events, movie and restaurant reviews, and local government meetings and actions. It also includes articles of interest and insight like Bill Dunn's 'When All is Said and Dunn', Dr. Jack Von Bulow's insightful information on dental and health topics and Pat Ostrye's 'memories'. But it was Dana's hometown of Temple City which benefitted the most from the newspaper. Whatever happened in the city, was usually mentioned somewhere in the paper. If you needed to know what took place, what was going to take place or who's who in the city, you only needed to read the weekly edition. And even though significant information and numerous activities relating to the other cities on the distribution circuit were included, it was the government notes, comments and editorials which were directly related to Temple City. One of my memories of Dana occurred this past June when he was trying to renew his contract with the City of Temple City. Another local newspaper had made a very attractive bid for the same contract and Dana appeared before the City Council to present his bid. He made a very clear, detailed and sincere presentation. He didn't criticize the other newspaper, he didn't offer excuses why he couldn't match an element of their bid, he just stated what his newspaper could do and what it had been doing over the years. The floor was then opened for public comment and I would guess 10-15 people came forward and criticized his newspaper as well as Dana himself. I watched him as he sat there. He seemed hurt, looked uneasy, but still sat calmly while only a few feet away from his criticizers. I sat there thinking something is wrong here, these people didn't know the real Dana, the hard work he put into the newspaper. They didn't see the benefit Dana and his newspaper was providing to them and the city. I had heard enough. My son was prodding me to step forward and when Mayor Wilson asked if anyone else had something to say; I stood and walked up to the podium to speak on Dana's and the newspapers behalf. Too often in life we're given an opportunity to speak up on something but for whatever reason we fail to take action. In retrospect, I'm so glad I stood up and supported my friend. It was the right thing to do. And little did I know that it would also be one of the last times I would see Dana.   I talked to him immediately after that city council meeting, as well as a couple of weeks later. I asked him about the criticism he received and he said, 'Joe, that wasn't nearly as bad as the meeting for the previous contract'. He never said anything negative about those who vented their complaints, he didn't refer to his criticizers' in offensive terms, and he didn't express any bitterness against them. That was the real Dana. To him, it was part of the job of running a newspaper and he accepted it as that. I've known Dana since 1994 but only started writing for him last October. I offered to write an 'historical related column' for him and provide his readers with a few stories of special interest. We met to discuss it and he shared with me his ideas. He told me what would work and what would not work. He also told me I'd have fun and my writing style would improve with each column. He offered me encouragement and suggested I cover sporting events. Every column I submitted, he published. He never pushed, he rarely changed anything. He was so easy to work for. And he was right, it was fun and I think my writing did improve. I can't thank Dana enough for the opportunity he gave me to write about my two passions: history and baseball. Without his friendship and support, I may never have been able to meet so many new people, visit numerous historical places and realize my dream visit to Dodger Stadium. Writing this column came at a difficult time in my life but in reality it was the perfect remedy, and I am so very thankful to Dana for providing that. As in most San Gabriel Valley cities, especially Temple City, streets were named by the original city founders after someone of significance. There are a number of streets in Temple City which I have been able to identify for whom they were named, but there are also many whose references have been hard to locate. Street names like Ancourt, Buttons, Degas and Roseglen, are all permanently integrated within the city street guide but the person who was named for them remains a mystery to most of us and their personal significance is unknown. The considerable contributions which Dana and his San Gabriel Valley Weekly newspaper have provided to this city for over 10 years are certainly worthy of special recognition. Perhaps someday, somewhere in this city, a new street will be planned, mapped and created. It will need a name and I suggest it be named after Dana. Call it Dana Drive or Baskin Avenue or Dana Baskin Court. Whatever name is chosen, it would be a fitting tribute to a man who did so much for so long for the city he cared about the most, the City of Temple City......

Chapter 24: 'Time Jockey' – *Ryan Tucker: His Story is Just Beginning* –

By Joe Castillo (08-28-08)

It is 7:38 AM Thursday morning July 10th and I'm walking my 2-plus miles at Temple City High School. I glance at the varsity baseball field and remember back to 2005. It was just 3 ½ years ago that Ryan Tucker was pitching in front of large gathering of scouts, photographers and fans. Tonight, Ryan and his Florida Marlins teammates visit the Dodgers in his first visit since being called up to the big leagues on June 8th. It's unbelievable how fast he has come in such a short time.

Ryan first appeared in the Marlin dugout almost 2 hours before game time. He seemed so much bigger than the last time I saw him but I think it's the fact he's in a Florida Marlin uniform. He was giving another interview and he seemed so relaxed and confident in his answers. He appeared very comfortable being interviewed and answering questions. We exchanged hugs and small talk, we took pictures together. After a few minutes, he politely excused himself to warm-up with his fellow pitchers and he asked us to come back afterwards. You could see and hear the enthusiasm and excitement in his voice; he's enjoying playing baseball and appeared to be quite content.

Ryan has changed quite a bit since I first met him 12 years ago but there is one thing besides his love of baseball that hasn't changed... his relationship with younger kids. You see, Ryan has always taken the time and energy to talk and help the younger kids, who always looked up to him. Ryan is a big kid himself but with a big heart. When he was a little league coach on the Major Mariners, I could see how he related to the players on their own level. And he was having fun doing it! When I saw him at Dodger Stadium on Thursday he was busy signing autographs before stretching, after stretching, in the bullpen and after the game. I don't know how many he signed but I bet it was more than any other Marlin, or Dodger for that matter.

I'm sure that Tim, Stacy and Meghan Tucker are extremely proud of Ryan and what he's achieved so far. They supported him throughout his career and have been beside him his entire journey. They gave him the best life, coaching, training and equipment in order for him to reach his goal. He never missed a practice that I can recall and he was always one of the first to arrive and last to leave.

Ryan has developed quite a following around Temple City and brought out about fifty of his friends and fans to Dodger Stadium on Thursday alone. Included in his cheering section were:

- Anthony Castillo, who managed/coached Ryan through Little League and soccer. Jason Castillo, a long-time teammate, was also in attendance;

- Sheehan Casey, TCHS Ram and TCALL Tiger teammate and friend;

- Kyle MacDonald, Ryan's very close and good friend;

- Brad MacDonald and his family;

- Nick Fetterhoff, TCHS teammate and friend;

- Jeremy Ortiz, fellow TCHS Ram and TCALL Tiger teammate;

- The O'Leary, Buccola, Harrison and Owens family, and a number of others.

In talking to him, his coaches and watching Ryan throughout the game, the following comments, thoughts and observations are included ....

__Praise__ ..... In my unbiased opinion, Ryan got off to a pretty solid major league start. That feeling was confirmed with Marlin Pitching Coach Mark Wiley, who provided an update on Ryan. Wiley said the best thing about Ryan was his competitiveness and his excellent arm action. 'He has a good temperament and we're going to find a spot for him in relief.' Wiley mentions that his number one pitch is the fastball but more work is needed on his change-up. When asked to appraise Ryan, Manager Fredi Gonzalez' eyes open wide and a smile crosses his face. 'He's something special …. We're trying to fit him into the bullpen and we couldn't be more pleased with him' says Gonzalez in his glowing appraisal. It is mentioned to Gonzalez that Ryan is a local kid from Temple City and will have a number of family and friends here to watch him. Gonzalez is quick to respond saying that 'he's sure Ryan will pitch sometime between now and Sunday.'

__Autographs__ …. As he came off the field after stretching, Ryan was the last Marlin to get to the dugout because he had been signing autographs along the right field foul line. One small boy got his attention and Ryan gladly went over and signed his baseball. Ryan walked away and immediately realized he still had the boy's pen. He called out to him and jogged over to return the pen. After doing my last interview with him, I asked Ryan to sign a couple of baseballs for my sons. He gladly signed them and even invited me to his house for an after-game gathering.

__In the Bullpen__…. An hour into the game, Ryan started to do his stretching. He was in a Marlins warm-up jersey and had yet to display his game jersey. Between the 5th and 6th innings, Ryan took off the warm-ups and began to throw in the bullpen. The Marlins get out and the Dodgers leave the field to bat, the gates to the right-field bullpen opened and out strolled Ryan. He jogged slowly to the edge of the infield dirt. From there he walked to the mound where he was met by Catcher Cody Ross. They talked a few seconds and Ross quickly jogged back to his position behind the plate.

__The Game__ … Ryan completed his warm-ups and was ready to face his first Dodger batter. The score was Marlins 4 – Dodgers 3 in the bottom of the 6th inning. Due up was the heart of the Dodgers lineup: Martin, Kent and Loney. At 9:05 PM, Ryan threw his first pitch to All-Star catcher Russell Martin, who is batting .298

with 9 home runs and 43 RBI's. Ryan's first pitch is a 96 MPH fastball for a strike followed by an 89 MPH breaking ball for ball one. With the count 1 and 1, Ryan throws a change-up and Martin connected, driving it into the left-field pavilion to tie the score at 4 runs apiece. Next up was Jeff Kent, who came to the plate and worked a full count. Finally, Kent hits a grounder back to Ryan for the first out. First baseman James Loney was next in the order and came in with a .302 batting average. Ryan started him with a 96 MPH fastball for a strike, a 90 MPH slider for a ball, a 90 MPH breaking ball which is fouled off. Ryan came back with an 86 MPH breaking ball which Loney swings at and misses to strikeout for the second out. Left Fielder Delwyn Young followed in the batting order. Ryan made six pitches to Young including a 98 MPH fastball strike to record a full count. Ryan throws a fastball and gets Young to ground out for the third and final out to end the inning. With an easy stride, Ryan walked off the mound to the dugout. His line score: 20 pitches, 12 K's, 8 balls, 1 run, 1 earned run, 1 inning.

    Postgame... Ryan had the following to say on his performance. On the pitch to Martin: 'It was a high change-up, a dumb pitch to make. If it was down, he would have hit a grounder'. On the mood of the Marlin's clubhouse: 'It's good... we're going to win it. We have a big series coming with Philadelphia and Atlanta at home'. On his performance: '.. even after the home run, we were still tied and with this team a number of guys can hit it out, just like tonight.' His comments show the competitiveness of this young man.

    Ryan has sure come a long way in a short time and his future looks very bright. As long as he keeps learning and playing with the same excitement and enthusiasm he's played with his entire career, he'll have a long and successful career. And I hope Ryan keeps signing all those autographs. It's good for baseball, fans and all those young kids who look up to Ryan and may have a dream of one day becoming a professional baseball player.

Chapter 25:   'Time Jockey' – *Ryan Tucker: Game Day* – By Joe Castillo (08-28-08)

Ryan Tucker, the 2005 graduate of Temple City High School and former Temple City American Little Leaguer, made his major league debut on Sunday June 8, 2008, pitching five solid innings and earning the victory in the Florida Marlins 9-3 win over the Cincinnati Reds. Tucker allowed one earned run and 2 hits while getting 6 strikeouts and walking five batters in his five complete innings of work.

Pitching at home against the fifth-place Reds, Tucker gave up a lead-off double to shortstop Jerry Hairston. He then got behind the count to centerfielder Jay Bruce but came back to strike him out. Ken Griffey Jr., seeking to become the 6th player to hit his 600th career home run, was intentionally walked to bring up Brandon Phillips. Even though a power pitcher, Tucker has throughout his career perfected pitching low strikes and induced Phillips to ground into an inning-ending double play.

In the second, Tucker again was challenged. He walked the leadoff hitter leftfielder Adam Dunn, stuck out Joey Votto and then hit Edwin Encarnacion after being ahead in the count 1-2. When former Dodger Catcher Cody Ross became Tucker's third strikeout victim, it looked like Tucker would escape without any damage. With the pitchers spot up, Tucker got behind the count to Aaron Harang. On a full-count pitch, the light hitting Harang lined a single into left field and drove in his first run of the 2008 season. Not yet out of trouble, Tucker settled down and induced Hairston into a fielder's choice groundout.

Thereafter, Tucker would settle down and dominate the 3rd, 4th and 5th innings. He pitched to 4 batters in the third, only giving up a walk to Griffey. In the 4th, he pitched a 1-2-3 inning, striking out Votto for the second time in the game. In the 5th, with one out Tucker walked Hairston and Bruce to bring up future Hall-Of-Famer Ken Griffey Jr. Even though only 21 years old, Tucker has always been a very knowledgeable and smart baseball player, and was not about to become an historical footnote in Griffeys' great baseball career. He worked carefully to the All-Star right-fielder keeping the ball down in strike zone and the strategy paid off as Griffey grounded into a fielder's choice. The next batter, Phillips, also grounded out and Tucker had once again baffled the Reds.

Tucker was replaced in the bottom of the 5th, leading 2-1, after giving the second-place Marlins a much needed boost by resting their struggling bullpen. After his major league debut, he is 1-0 with a very impressive 1.80 ERA and allowing opposing batters an average of .118. He started the season with the AA Carolina Mudcats, going 4-1 with a 1.41 ERA in 21 innings.

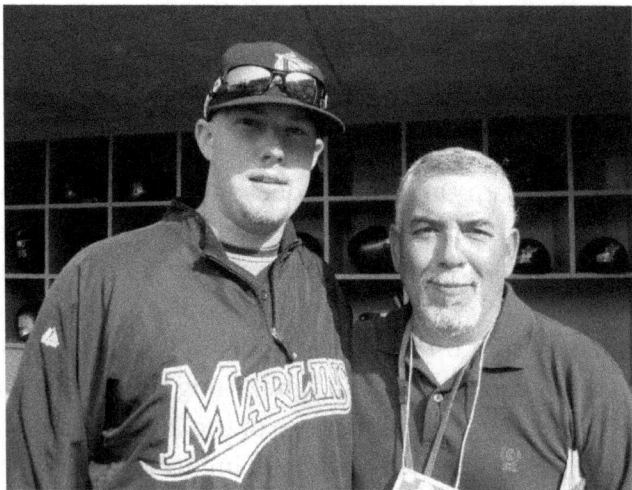

www.ingramcontent.com/pod-product-compliance
Lightning Source LLC
Chambersburg PA
CBHW061456040426
42450CB00008B/1381